"A splendidly vivid account of ...
today – ideal for new Christ...
perhaps, through one of the m...
that are now springing up. Rob is a wonderful storyteller. This book is a real gift."

– Revd Dr Michael Moynagh, author of *Being Church, Doing Life*

"This book hits the spiritual spot and offers strategies by which every follower can become an agent of change for God's Kingdom come! Don't just read it – live it!"

– Major Danielle Strickland, author of *The Liberating Truth*

"We really are citizens of a different Kingdom. It's an upside down kingdom full of wonder, beauty and glorious amazement. Rob captures God's passion for people, communities and the need for unity in the bride of Christ's body. Rob is an authentic Jesus lover – trust me, you will love this book."

– Cris Rogers, speaker, pastor and church visionary, author of *The Bible Book by Book*

"I love this book because it is so inspirational. As you read it you'll be reminded of what it really means to be a citizen of God's Kingdom and the unique part you play in building His Kingdom on the earth."

– Wendy Beech-Ward, Events and Ambassadors Director, Compassion UK

"A refreshingly honest, vibrant account of a young man set on living a Gospel-inspired life. He's one of a new breed. Rob's eyeballing the religious infrastructures and comfortable belief-systems of our day, and humbly asserting that there's more, oh so much more, if we would but be brave enough to step into a fresh reality. A Kingdom reality. A call to true Citizenship."

– Tania Bright-Cook, Chair of Love 146 Europe

"Anyone who knows Rob knows that he follows Jesus, wherever that leads him. This book could save you from the many dead-ends that can prevent us from embracing true discipleship. Being a citizen of heaven trumps all earthly allegiances and identities, and settling for anything less is missing out on the purpose for which you were created."

– Paul Harcourt, Vicar of All Saints' Woodford Wells and New Wine Regional Director for London and East

"Citizen points to every person who deeply desires to follow Jesus. Rob brings clear perspectives on what it means to follow Jesus, take risks and live with a unique identity as a citizen of the everlasting Kingdom."

– Chris McFarland, Executive Director, PULSE

"With heartfelt stories and sound scriptural truths, Rob shares his journey of rediscovering the Kingdom of God and our role as its citizens. He challenges our erroneous notions of part-time, self-styled Christianity, urging us to offer our full allegiance not to ourselves or to an organization, but to the King."

– Ben Armacost, author of Bridge to the Beautiful City

"Will force you to ask questions and confront deeply held ideas about what it is to live in and live for the Kingdom. If you are satisfied and comfortable with your current state of life and faith, then I suggest you put this book down and continue shopping."

– Wes Hamilton, Lead Pastor, Hulen Street Church, Fort Worth, TX

"I have enjoyed reading Rob's story and chuckled at his tales of cultural navigation. I identify with his journey and find his thoughts on identity and citizenship both challenging and encouraging. This is not a 'stay in your comfort zone' book.

The story for Rob and the Awaken Movement does not finish at the end of this book and I look forward to watching (and collaborating) as it all unfolds further."

– Stu Garrard, One Sonic Society, formerly of Delirious?

"This book is counter-cultural. A manifesto. A call to awaken to a global rather than a territorial citizenship. The author – an American citizen – exemplifies this call by exchanging a pulpit in front of thousands at an exalted Texas mega-church for a small inner-city community in London. And yet, in the midst of this seismic culture-shift, finds himself living dreams fully awake, with a heart overflowing with beauty and joy."

– Randy Elrod, CEO and Founder, Creative Community and author of *A Renaissance Redneck In A Mega-Church Pulpit and Sex, Lies & Religion*

"Through biblical exploration, historical survey, and vivid illustration, Rob Peabody paints a picture of what being a citizen of God's kingdom looks like in this world: a citizenship from heaven but radically rooted to earth, as risky in self sacrifice as it is compassionate in tone, a citizenship of humble allegiance to the One who taught radical love of neighbor."

– Sheridan Voysey, writer, speaker, broadcaster, and author of *Resurrection Year: Turning Broken Dreams into New Beginnings*

About the Author

Rob Peabody serves as the co-founder and director of Awaken, a non-profit charity that exists to resource the church for action. In 2011, Rob, along with his wife, Medea, and their two boys, left his position as lead campus pastor of a megachurch in Texas to pioneer and lead fresh expressions of church seeking to engage unreached 20s and 30s in northeast London. This work is commissioned by the International Mission Board of the SBC and in partnership with the Church of England. Rob currently serves as a missional consultant for multiple church networks in the UK, is a member of the Speaking Team at Spring Harvest, and is charged with casting vision and leading a new upcoming national UK 18–30's conference, The Pursuit. Beyond speaking at conferences in the US and UK, Rob has also written a small group film series entitled *Kingdom Rise*, released March 2013.

CITIZEN

Your role in the alternative kingdom

ROB PEABODY

MONARCH
BOOKS
Oxford, UK, and Grand Rapids, Michigan, USA

Published by Monarch Books
an imprint of
Lion Hudson plc
Wilkinson House, Jordan Hill Road,
Oxford OX2 8DR, England
Email: monarch@lionhudson.com
www.lionhudson.com/monarch

ISBN 978 0 85721 542 0
e-ISBN 978 0 85721 543 7

First edition 2014

Acknowledgments
Scripture quotations marked "NIV" are taken from the Holy Bible, New
International Version, copyright © 1979, 1984, 2011 Biblica, formerly International
Bible Society. All rights reserved. "NIV" is a registered trademark of Biblica UK
trademark number 1448790. Scripture quotations marked The Message taken
from The Message. Copyright © by Eugene H. Peterson 1993, 1994, 1995, 1996,
2000, 2001, 2002. Used by permission of NavPress Publishing Group. Scripture
quotations marked AKJV are taken from the American King James Version,
produced by Stone Engelbrite and in the public domain. Scripture quotations
marked NASB taken from the New American Standard Bible®, Copyright ©
1960, 1962, 1963, 1968, 1971, 1972, 1973, 1975, 1977, 1995 by The Lockman
Foundation. Used by permission. Scripture quotations marked ESV are from The
Holy Bible, English Standard Version® (ESV®) copyright © 2001 by Crossway,
a publishing ministry of Good News Publishers. All rights reserved. Scripture
quotations marked RSV are from The Revised Standard Version of the Bible
copyright © 1346, 1952 and 1971 by the Division of Christian Education of
the National Council of Churches in the USA. Used by permission. All Rights
Reserved. Quotations designated NET are from the NET Bible® copyright ©1996-
2006 by Biblical Studies Press, L.L.C. http://bible.org All rights reserved. Scripture
quoted by permission.

A catalogue record for this book is available from the British Library

Printed and bound in the UK, June 2014, LH26

To Medea,

Whom I love with a passion that time only

strengthens.

You are my beloved bride and best friend,

and there is no one I would rather be on this

journey with than you.

Contents

Acknowledgments

This book was not written alone. The words within it represent experiences, conversations, ideas, friendships, risks, struggles, regrets, fears, hopes, and prayers. All of which have been caught up in God's immeasurable grace and blessing that has been poured out over this season of my life.

This is the first full-length book I have published, and it must be said that it would not have been so had the loved ones in my life not been so sacrificial, loving, and selfless. My wife, Medea, and my two boys, Liam and Tate, are my love and joy. Thank you for freeing me up to dream and write, and sacrificing so that God's message in these pages could be delivered through me. Your love and support is far greater than I deserve.

A huge gratitude-filled thanks to my parents, Bob and Jane. The older I get, the more aware I become of the sacrifice and commitment you gave in raising your children in a way that points them to Jesus. To Drew and Lindsay, Joel and Allison, and Laura Jane, it is an honor and a joy to call you family. To Janine, your love, encouragement, and practical support have helped us so much on this journey.

Many of the ideas and thoughts in this book came about through conversations with my greatest friends. Life on life, they have been the community that God uses to refine. Matt and Lauren Larsen, Matt and Deanna Wheeler, Andrew and (now) Megan Shepherd, thank you for loving and believing in me.

To my long-time mentor and friend, Robert Turner: you have taught me so much, given me the confidence to be me, have always stood in my corner, and made it possible for us to move to London.

To Joel Warren, my partner and fellow dreamer for Awaken, and all of the Awaken team – Vanessa and Mark Warren, Angie and Dustin Eddy, Hai Phung, and Kat Davis – you guys are the absolute best.

Thank you for embracing me, showing love and support, and joyfully sending us out people of Lake Pointe Firewheel. To my Awaken London crew and our missional communities, thanks for bearing with me during this season of writing. You are so much fun, and it is an honor to call you brothers and sisters. A huge debt of gratitude is owed to the International Mission Board for allowing me the freedom to work "outside of the box" and for being a constant source of encouragement and blessing to me and the ministry God has given.

I am so grateful for the many coffees shared in London with my good friend and mentor, Andy Martin. Thanks for whole-heartedly following Jesus and opening your life to me.

Many thanks to all of the friends who gave commendations for *Citizen*. I am honored that you would give such praise of this work.

Tony Collins, Jenny Ward, and the editorial team at Monarch, without you, this book would not be fit to read! Thanks for believing in and pushing me to write, Tony. I am privileged to be able to work alongside you all.

And finally, I have learned so much from my brothers and sisters "across the pond". Wendy Beech-Ward, Cris Rogers, and Paul Harcourt, you took us in when we were orphaned in our new city and lavished us with the love and grace of God. Your open arms and sincere friendship have modeled for me what it means to be a citizen of the Kingdom.

Preface

A Citizen's Awakening

Jerusalem – March 2008

Sitting out on the balcony of our hotel overlooking the Temple Mount and the Old City of Jerusalem, I experienced a moment of clarity that, unbeknown to me at the time, would change the course of my life.

This vision, calling, supernatural moment of God-given clarity – whatever you are comfortable calling it – was very clear that night, and it was so fitting that it occurred in the "Holy City." For centuries this special city was drawn on maps as the very center of the world. This was the place where the presence of the Lord resided in the Temple within the city gates, the city that for the people of Israel was their prize and possession, and the city where the King of the universe was murdered ... and on this night, it was a place of breakthrough for me.

My friend and mentor, Robert, had brought me to Jerusalem for a guys' sightseeing adventure, and we had definitely enjoyed ourselves in Israel. A few days in Galilee, an afternoon floating on the Dead Sea, and a bit more time spent exploring the centuries of history in the ancient city were all coming to an end. And here we were on our last night in the country taking some time to reflect, share, and open our hearts in a way that never quite seems possible amidst the routine and demands of "normal" life at home.

Back home in Dallas, Texas, I was a twenty-six-year-old pastor at a mega-church who was newly married and had just graduated with my Master's degree from seminary. Put simply, I was in way over my head. I had left university with an undergraduate degree in business and had felt a leading (through a number of different circumstances) into full-time vocational ministry. So, with a diploma in my hand, I moved back home to Dallas and took a job as a summer youth intern in one of the nation's largest churches. I realized two things that summer: one – there is no way that I could survive more than a summer as a youth pastor, and two (a little more edifying) – I was falling in love with the local church.

The next autumn found me enrolled as a Master's student at our local seminary and serving at that same church as the university minister, working predominately with young people aged eighteen to twenty-five. For the next three years I walked the tightrope of balancing classes and ministry, found the best friends whom I still cherish to this day, married my beloved wife, and started to learn what it looks like to serve others and point people to Jesus amidst the brokenness and baggage that we all inevitably end up carrying. It was amazing. I still look back at those years and consider them the best of my young life.

Upon graduating from seminary, I was pulled into our senior pastor's office and given an opportunity that completely blindsided me. The offer was this: move to the church's newest community campus (think church plant on steroids) and lead the efforts there as pastor of a new church full of young families, and be mentored in the process.

"Are you serious? You want *me* to lead this new church? I'm so young; are you sure?" After some heavy reassurance and confidence bestowed by our pastor, I was off to serve all the generations at this new church – not just university students.

It was weird at first. I was twenty-six, the youngest on the staff team, yet the supervisor of them all. I still consider it a heavy dose of grace that God placed me with such a humble and honoring team on this campus, who overlooked my youth and lack of experience and believed in me and the mission God was calling us to as a church. Our first Sunday brought in close to 2,000 people. So many showed up that we had to place them in "overflow" seats in the hallways while they watched what happened in the worship center via video. I quickly learned how to manage the crowds and work the systems so that we could accommodate such a large number of people in worship each week and maximize our staff and worship space. We were off to an amazing start. It was incredible that so many people were encountering Jesus each week and being changed by His power and gospel… and then it got messy.

I lasted for about a year.

The exhilaration of seeing so many people encounter and worship God each week, the numerous small-group Bible studies that we were starting, and the adrenaline rush of Sunday-morning worship made it all seem more than worthwhile. But no matter how many people encountered God each weekend, how much affirmation our team received, how many people walked through the doors of our church during the week, and how much life change was reported, I felt this nagging uneasiness that I was selling out.

This all came out during our conversation on the rooftop in Jerusalem.

As Robert and I discussed, dissected, and analyzed what was going on and where I was at, it became clear that I was not satisfied with what I was inevitably devoting my life to. I was essentially getting paid to manage a staff, run executive management for a church campus, and be the up-front face of a mega-church system in the buckle of the Bible Belt. Don't get me wrong – there is nothing wrong with the seeker-sensitive, attractional model of church. Indeed, God is using it to accomplish amazing things for His glory. But, for me, there was something missing that my soul craved. And as we talked that night, overlooking the Dome of the Rock and the eerie golden tint that it projects onto the night sky, I knew that something had to change. I couldn't carry on in this way.

Robert continued to ask thought-provoking questions that felt like blades aimed directly at my heart. Not blades that were intended to cause harm, but the more gentle sculpting kind that we all need to have directed our way from time to time. As we cut our way down to the core of who God had uniquely created me to be – the skills, passions, giftings, desires, hopes, and dreams – it finally all came together for the first time.

God was giving me a vision for His church, a vision that later came to be known as the Awaken Movement.

Upon returning to Dallas and re-engaging in my normal routine, I found myself one day in our worship leader's office, sharing this newly discovered vision. Joel and his twin brother, Mark, had started a band that had toured much of the U.S. in the early 2000s as a Christian worship band, but had reduced the amount of traveling and playing to focus on their families and serve the local church. Joel and I were becoming great friends, and shared many passions, burdens, and views on life and the church. This specific day in Joel's office, he began to tell me about his most recent trip to South Africa. Joel explained to me that, somewhere amidst serving the poor in Port Shepstone and worshiping with local believers from a thriving church in the city, he had had a revelation that he had known about for a long time, but which had never been shown to him in this way before. He described the disparity between the "Haves" in the city and this specific church, and the "Have Nots" just across town.

I remember him recounting how the people across town had nothing: they lived in an impoverished box (shanty) town that was racially and socioeconomically segregated from the "Haves" across the way. Joel's heart was broken by this injustice and he was racking his brain trying to figure out what he could do to make a difference in the lives of these people, to be a part of the solution. As he poured out his heart in divulging the details of this most recent experience in South Africa, his longing to be used in our church context in the suburbs of Dallas for something greater than his current position, and his God-given experiences with music in the past, something clicked.

God was awakening not just one heart, but two…

So here we were, two young guys leading a mega-church community campus in a middle–upper-class suburb, with a new multi-million-dollar building, a mass of people, and an uneasiness that there was more to be learned and taught about what it looks like to follow Jesus on our patch. We decided then and there in Joel's office that God was granting vision and clarity to both of us, and it was high time that we moved on from mulling over our joint frustrations to action. This newfound passion and insight into the gospel of Jesus was transforming us so that we were no longer satisfied with the status quo. The Spirit was laying out the pieces of the puzzle and fitting them together in a way we had never seen or experienced before. We were ready to shake things up both in our lives and in the lives of the people in the church. God was instilling in us a holy discontent and calling us to live for more, to be part of seeing change in our community, to get caught up in something so much greater than our individual lives, and to lead people to see Jesus honored from Monday to Saturday and not just for an hour on Sunday in our worship services. It was time to get uncomfortable.

We scheduled a meeting with the mayor of our community and told him about our new local church, explaining who we were and then asking him a pointed question: "What do *you* see as the greatest needs in our community?" We further explained that, as followers of Jesus, we were meant to be passionate about what He is passionate about, and that we were learning as a church that we should be disadvantaging ourselves for the benefit of others. We expressed our hope of beginning to play a part in righting the wrongs of sin and injustice in our community, but admitted that, in our current state, we were fairly closed-minded and oblivious to the needs around us.

You could tell that we had caught him off guard. He looked briefly around the room and then, in a very matter-of-fact way, said, "Do you realize there is a Title 1 school two miles from your church?"

"No," we replied, quickly followed up by, "What is a Title 1 school?" He went on to explain that a Title 1 school in the State of Texas is one in which at least eighty percent of the student population is on government assistance. Owing to the poverty levels of the families it caters for, a Title 1 school is provided with federal funding as a means of preventing "at-risk" children from falling behind academically. We ended our time with the mayor by offering our help and support to the community and adding that we would try to develop a relationship with this nearby school. We told him of our desire as followers of Jesus to begin meeting these needs, and that the church should (and now would) be actively involved in addressing the concerns that came across his desk.

As Joel and I left our meeting with the mayor, we discussed the fact that, as individuals and as a church, we felt we had become blinded to the issues and needs right in front of us in an effort to win the world. In effect, we had "missed our Jerusalem." You see, as a church, we were doing a lot of great things. People were attending worship services by the thousand, many were "being saved," and people were taking a step forward in their relationship with God through baptism; discipleship programs were being led, Bible studies formed, and youth activities attended, and prayer ministry was taking place. We had a strong presence in China, South Africa, Russia, and other faraway countries, giving financial support, sending mission teams, and coaching people. But it now dawned on us that, despite all of this busy ministry within the church, when we looked across the street or two miles down the road, we were overlooking the needs and injustices in our own area. We had very little contact with anyone in our community who did not look, act, or behave the way we did. God was opening our eyes to the sobering reality that we had missed our "Jerusalem."

In Acts 1:8, after Jesus' crucifixion and resurrection, He is with His disciples for forty days, teaching and showing them signs of the resurrection life, before He ascends to heaven to sit at the right hand of the Father. His last words on earth are: "You will receive power when the Holy Spirit comes on you; and you will be my witnesses in Jerusalem, and in all Judea and Samaria, and to the ends of the earth."[1]

With this new God-given realization, we sat down with the principal of this nearby underprivileged school, who turned out to be a friend of a friend and a fellow follower of Jesus. God had definitely set this up. Chris had been serving as a small-group leader at our central church location. He welcomed us in, loved the idea, and facilitated a relationship

1   Acts 1:8 (NIV).

between our campus and his elementary school. We were off and running. A year later, as a church we were supporting the families connected to the school by running financial counseling seminars, mentoring initiatives, school clean-up days, and family fun days, donating school supplies, Christmas gifts and meals, coaching soccer teams for boys whose dads were not involved in their lives, undertaking landscaping projects, and offering encouragement to the teachers and other staff – anything we could do to play a part in alleviating the brokenness that this school represented for this cross section of the community. What made this different from the humanitarian efforts or government involvement that the school had seen in the past is that we did it because of the love of Jesus, in the power of Jesus, and for the name of Jesus, with no expectation of any form of payoff or credit because of the work.

We tried to play an active part in the lives of the families of this school and what ensued was the reclaiming of our "Jerusalem" for our church. We were engaged in an awakening (on a small suburban level) of the people of our church, and we were learning that when Jesus steps into our lives and begins to transform who we are through the power of the gospel, we in turn are released and sent out to engage with and transform the community around us. It was so life-giving.

Joel and I continued to envision an awakening of people's hearts and lives to the greater story of what Jesus was up to in the Gospels. Somewhere along the road that is evangelicalism in the Western world, we have either heard or been taught a gospel of individualism, or what I like to refer to as "Golden Ticket Theology" (think *Willy Wonka and the Chocolate Factory*).[2] There are many different variations and streams of this gospel, but it generally goes something like this:

> You were born into a sinful and broken world, which is bad, and you are a sinner. God is good and has a wonderful plan for your life. You need to trust Jesus so that you can go to heaven when you die.
> *– Person trusts Jesus and receives salvation –*
> Now that you are saved from hell you need to learn to start sinning less while you wait either to die or for Jesus to come back (whichever comes first), so that you can escape this bad, sinful world. Go to church, be a good person like Jesus, and if it comes up and you are comfortable with it, tell the other poor people who don't know what you do how they can escape hell too.

Of course it was never spelled out this way and I am somewhat oversimplifying, but this was the essence of the functional gospel that I had learned about while growing

2   *Willy Wonka and the Chocolate Factory*, Warner Bros (USA), 30 June 1971.

up, and which countless others still believe today. When we mix the egocentrism that is a cultural staple in the Western world, in which the individual "I" functions as the center of the universe, with a gospel of "If I died today, where would I go?", this is the most logical and probable theology that develops.

Let's set out a hypothetical scenario with a man named Frank, using this pervasive theology that we find in the West.

Frank is a great guy. He married his university sweetheart right after graduation and has two young kids. He has a good job in the city and a nice house in the suburbs, goes to church every week, and is involved in a home group with his wife and other young married couples, where the kids go along and play while the adults have a Bible study. In his spare time, he coaches his son's football team, works on the house, and plans family holidays, all the while watching his financial portfolio in order to provide in the best possible way for his family. Outsiders would look at Frank's life and say that he was a great family man, a good neighbor, and a moral person. Squeaky clean – not very much you could get mad at him about.

Frank goes to church, tithes to the church, is involved in a small group in the church, and even talks to people about his church when asked. But when you start digging deeper, below the surface, most of the things Frank does are either cultural norms, or what he would be doing anyway.

His unspoken priorities are being comfortable, pursuing security for himself and his loved ones, and raising his family properly. Frank mostly hangs out with people like himself, people whom he understands and can relate to, and is somewhat uneasy (even fearful) when forced to be in new situations or to mix with others outside his "world." At the end of the day, as long as he and the people he cares deeply for are taken care of and happy, he is content. He knows where he is going when he dies, is raising his children in the church, and along the way is trying to be the best Frank he can be.

Frank is an amazing guy, but there is a problem with Frank.

Frank doesn't get it. He has not allowed Jesus' gospel to permeate his being. Instead, Jesus has become an add-on when Frank has run out of options on his own, a go-to in times of trouble. Frank is trying to live the "Western dream" and bring Jesus along for the ride as well. His unspoken mantra is "Be a good moral person, sin less, take care of your family, and you will be taken care of by God." According to Frank, God is a moral, white, middle–upper-class guy who lives in the suburbs, doesn't drink, and votes Republican.

Sadly, Frank represents the majority of people I have met in the church in the West.

Would Jesus and Frank be friends? My assumption is that Jesus would befriend Frank at first, but, in time, He would ask more of Frank than he was comfortable with giving, and soon enough Frank would go back to managing his 401k.

When we first hear about the good news of Jesus and how we, in our sinful brokenness, can be reconciled to the righteous God of the universe by faith in the work of Christ on the cross, we encounter the most incredible news in the history of existence. By God's grace, we become partakers in eternal life with Him. This gospel brings life, restoration, relationship with God, and heaven. The mystery of God that has been revealed to us gives us a future and a hope, and in this we find joy and peace. But, all too often, salvation can become the Golden Ticket in our lives. It can be reduced to a "Get out of hell free card" (think Monopoly), which, once received, gives us eternal life, and then we end up in a holding pattern, waiting to die or for Jesus to return so that we can redeem our free ticket to heaven. Sure, we may do some nice things in our seventy to eighty years (God willing) on this planet, but what we are really banking on, what we are really looking forward to, is the moment when we get to escape this godless society full of pain and suffering, to share eternity with our Maker. Not a bad thing to look forward to at all. However, this kind of thinking is only half the story.

If the Christian life is only about escaping this world when we die, then I have an idea. Here's what we should do. When people come forward for baptism, we should do them a favor. The minister should ask the new believer if it is their testimony that they have placed their faith and trust in Jesus for the forgiveness of sins, and then he or she should gently put them under the water – and hold them there – till the bubbles stop! The way I see it, if life with Jesus is all about escaping the world, then the most loving thing we can do for people is to send them straight out of it and on to heaven.

Yes, Jesus died to save you *from* something (hell and eternal separation from Him), but He also died to save you *for* something.

And it is in the *for* something that Jesus invites us to add action to our faith. A quick glance through much of the New Testament and all of Paul's letters reinforces this point. We find that these writings not only speak of our future life with God in eternity, but also speak very practically and realistically about the resurrection life that we are now invited into through our salvation. In Colossians 3:3, Paul reminds us that we have died, and our lives are "now hidden with Christ in God."[3] Paul is being very clear here: you, follower of Jesus, are no longer the old you. You have been fundamentally changed, endowed with Christ's righteousness, restored, brought from death to life, and made new, and are in the process of being transformed into the image of Jesus.[4] And it is in this process of transformation, in which you grow and become more and more like Jesus,

3   Colossians 3:3 (NIV).
4   Ephesians 2:4–5; Romans 6:5–10.

that you take on His resurrection life and live as resurrected people in a world that is far from Him. Practically speaking, transformed people transform things. I fully believe that the Enemy would delight in nothing more than congregation upon congregation of professed Christians going through the motions, ticking the boxes of attending church, singing the songs, talking the talk, and then going home Sunday after Sunday with a pat on the back and little to no change in the way that they live during the rest of the week. This is not what Jesus died for! God did not subject Himself to humiliation, torture, and crucifixion so that His bride could meet in His name, and then leave impotent with regard to impact on the world.

The Jesus of the Gospels is calling us to so much more.

I now find myself living with my family in London, England. It's been five years since my Jerusalem rooftop experience. We have left our beloved family and friends, our community, our church, in a sense our identity, our comforts, and our thorough understanding of a culture as insiders back in the United States. We made the move to the UK in January 2011 to follow the call that Jesus has on our lives. He is worth it. I don't want to be like Frank – I know I easily could be. But the greater joy, I am finding, lies in complete abandonment to Jesus and His Spirit's leading.

We moved to London to lead Awaken in a post-Christian missional context. That basically means that we are seeking to follow and live out Jesus' way of life among people who are far from God and who would never set foot in a traditional church, and invite them into a community that "does life" together as the people of God. It is within this community that we debunk and deconstruct their preconceptions of a church and a religion that they don't really know much about (other than the fact that they reject it), and then reconstruct a biblical view of Jesus and His bride.

We lead different missional communities throughout the week in London, and the rest of our time is devoted to spearheading the efforts of the Awaken Movement. What started with a local church congregation opening their eyes and waking up to the needs in the community around them in the suburbs of Dallas led to a few more churches with a heart to move beyond their walls and do the same. Pretty soon, we realized that the Spirit was moving and had been bubbling up and creating this tension in countless others. As I write, I am overwhelmed by what God is piecing together – from Dallas to Nashville to New York to London to mainland Europe, a collective of compelled and talented musicians, pastors, photographers, designers, filmmakers, songwriters, authors, students, businessmen and -women, and missionaries, all with a passion to be part of a new creative approach to bringing together the needs of our broken cities and the change that bursts forth from a renewed community – the church. Out of all these people's efforts, the Awaken Movement was born with a desire to come alongside the local church and provide it with resources for action.[5] Our hope and desire is to see a generation of churchgoers inspired by the gospel to live as agents of change right where they are in their communities and cities.

You might be thinking, "That's all well and good, but that's not for me right now… that's not where I am." And if that is where you find yourself at this moment, I can relate to it. I've been there myself. Over the past five years, I have met countless believers who feel stuck in their attempt to live the Christian life. The life that Jesus has called them to and the life that they are currently living don't match up. Don't get me wrong: they want it to. They want the abundant life that the Gospels speak of, but in the church they currently attend, with the friends they surround themselves with, with the lifestyle they are pursuing, it doesn't come easily. And after a few failed attempts they settle for mediocrity in their relationship with Jesus.

After all, we have heaven in the bag. Anything else that could come from this relationship is just a bonus, right? At times we will feel guilt, frustration, uneasiness, dissatisfaction, and lack of fulfillment. These emotions subside, but we can't ever get rid of them completely. They

5   More info at: http://awakenmovement.com

are always lurking in the depths of our souls, because God won't give up on us. We know deep down that there has got to be more. We may not know how to find it, but we have hope that it is possible.

Have *you* ever felt this way?

You are not alone.

It is time to reclaim *your* "Jerusalem." I know that you may not know how to, and that's OK. It's not by accident that you are holding this book, and my prayer is that God will use it to take you on a journey that will begin to put some of the pieces together. There is an awakening happening in the church in the West. From the United States to the United Kingdom and into mainland Europe, God's Spirit is moving hearts to never again be satisfied with status-quo Christianity. This movement is not led by a personality or a strategy, but by the God of the universe Himself.

It will take a reimagining of your life, a repositioning of what you value, a re-identifying of who you are, and a recentering on the true King of the world. It will be hard at times, then sweetly exhilarating and right at others. In the end, you will find the life that you were created to live: a life so extraordinary and full of joy that you cannot even fully comprehend it right now; a life not wasted, a life that goes beyond just you, and a life that gives worship and glory to the One who is worthy. The Father is standing with open arms, inviting you in to experience all that He has created and called you to be. You have been saved for this, and now it is time to claim it.

> "I came so they can have real and eternal life,
> more and better life than they ever dreamed of."
>
> **Jesus**[6]

Rob Peabody
London

---

6   John 10:10 (*The Message*).

1

A Citizen's Identity

"We know what we are, but not what we may be."

William Shakespeare[7]

"If you'd asked anybody in the Roman Empire, from Germany to Egypt, from Spain to Syria, who the 'son of god' might be, the obvious answer, the politically correct answer, would have been 'Octavian'."

Tom Wright [8]

I have been living as a foreigner in a different kingdom for the past three years. On January 2, 2011, my wife, Medea, and I, along with our son, Liam, drove to the airport escorted

7　William Shakespeare, *Hamlet*.
8　Tom Wright, *Simply Jesus: Who He Was, What He Did, Why It Matters*, SPCK, 2011, p. 29.

by our family with a one-way ticket to the United Kingdom. We had sold every material thing we owned except for the belongings that would fit into suitcases and some large containers that could go in the baggage compartment of the plane. We had left behind our home, our cars, the dogs, furniture, our jobs, and, most importantly, the relationships that had formed a large part of who we were and still are to this day. As we stepped through security and into the terminal, we reminded ourselves that these loved ones were not gone, but just further away. As I looked over at my wife, I could sense that she was feeling the same as me: excited, nervous, unsure yet confident that this was what we were supposed to be doing; adventurous, hopeful, and alone.

We had been preparing for this moment for the past year, but it didn't change the fact that when we finally stepped out and acted on our decision a certain degree of anxiety came with it. Add to all those emotions the fact that a week earlier we had found out that we were expecting our second child (Tate), just as we were finalizing all our arrangements amidst the craziness of packing to move 4,759 miles across the pond. Needless to say, it was a bit of a hectic week.

London was cold, gray, and dreary when we arrived at Heathrow that morning… imagine that! Luckily we had bought our first proper winter coats, something I had never had a reason to own in the previous twenty-nine years of my life, before leaving Texas. After having had little to no sleep during the night on the plane (try telling a two-year-old that he is supposed to go night-night sitting upright surrounded by strangers), and with our new coats on, all our earthly belongings strewn across multiple luggage trolleys, and a jittery excitement at all that was new, we were on our way to our new home. We arrived, tried to figure out how to work a radiator, and immediately passed out from exhaustion after the previous day's ordeals.

Days turned into weeks, weeks into months, and the promise of some sort of spring was all we could hang on to when we hadn't seen the sun in what felt like forever. Note to those reading: if you live in a sunny climate and plan on moving to a cold, northern climate, don't do it in the dead of winter. Trust me. Vitamin D deficiency and seasonal depression are very real things. Actually, it wasn't quite as bad as it sounds. Once we learned how to layer our clothes, drink tea, and bought rainproof boots, everything was much more pleasant.

When I look back now, my first year of living in a new city, among new people, in a country that was not my own, was a time of processing and dealing with stated and unstated expectations. I didn't realize how many unspoken expectations had traveled with us on that plane. This first year in London was a time of searching and re-understanding... everything. I've explained it this way before: imagine waking up one morning in a new home in a new community, with no friends and no understanding of how things work in this new world in which you find yourself. You would probably begin to operate and order your new life based on what worked and didn't work in your previous one, but when you figure out that your new land is similar, but at the same time very different, it can leave you curious and excited for a while, but once that subsides, you can easily find yourself feeling frustrated and misunderstood.

This is what happened to me.

Many people graciously sat down with me and tried to help me make sense of what it means to live on the other side of "two nations divided by a common language," for which I am very thankful. But no one could really help me explain to Londoners who I am or what I do. Let me explain. In the "Bible Belt" of America, it is still an honorable and somewhat prestigious position to be an ordained minister in the church. People want to meet with you and value time spent with you; they feel as if you help them learn and understand more about God, and in turn, they love and take care of you. In fact, I'm ashamed to say I have played the "pastor" card on more than one occasion back home to get out of sticky situations or to ask for special favors, and it always worked. Being a pastor in Texas was a good thing, an honorable thing, and in many circles could even become a celebrity cult-of-personality thing. In Western Europe, not so much.

I tried identifying myself as a minister in England, but quickly realized that being seen as the first American government minister in the UK, although humorous, didn't actually explain correctly who I was or what I did. Next I tried "pastor," which doesn't really translate in a post-Christian society. "Like a vicar" sort of explained my role, but no one could get past my not being sixty-five, wearing a collar, and dressing "trendy" (their words, not mine). After many other failed attempts, the best of which was international spy, I settled on being the director of a Christian charity called Awaken. And by the end of year one, I loved the city, appreciated her people, and realized I was having an identity crisis.

Something happened when we set up our lives in a new country. Our perspective changed. The bubble I had lived and played in for my entire life in a single city in Texas had been popped, and now, for the first time, I was able to look with fresh eyes not only at my new city, but also at the one from which I had come. Leaning into this new perspective and then analyzing what it required of my life raised a number of questions that I had not really dealt with before. Do I think the things I think, believe the way I believe, and act the way I do because:

A) I am an American?

B) I am an American Christian?

C) I am a Christian (regardless of my citizenship)?

As I began to work through these different scenarios, it became very clear to me that the way I thought, believed, and acted was a big mix of all three categories. My worldview had been shaped by living in Texas, being raised and attending church in the "Bible Belt," and learning and trying to implement the life and teachings of Jesus as one of His followers. Back home, all this was normal. I just went about my day making decisions, having conversations, and living life in a way that was sociably acceptable and encouraged by others who looked, thought, and acted pretty much as I did – people whose lives were somewhat similar to mine. As a serious follower of Jesus, a seminary graduate, and a "professional Christian," I sincerely hoped that my worldview was continually being shaped by Jesus – that it was the foundation upon which other facets of my life and the lenses through which I viewed the world rested.

But, as I began having conversations in London with those far from the church who had no understanding of my faith – and effectively *could not* understand because they had never been in my previous world – I realized that my worldview and identity were being seen through each one of the above-mentioned lenses. No matter how hard we try to see things only from the perspective of "What would Jesus do?", our historical and personal context helps to interpret and answer that question for us. Therefore, simply asking what Jesus would do is a relative question that will be answered on the basis of the perspective these lenses bring.

These issues of worldview really come into play when we begin to examine Jesus in the Gospels. What did Jesus really mean when He said that the "Son of Man did not come to be served, but to serve?"[9] What did He want the people to hear when He prayed, "Your kingdom come, your will be done, on earth as it is in heaven?"[10] Why did the Jews think the way they did when Jesus showed up healing on the Sabbath, rebuking their esteemed officials, and seemingly disregarding the rules and customs of the Jewish faith that had been followed for thousands of years? Why was it that the Romans eventually executed Him in the same manner that they would use to rid themselves of a status-seeking slave or an attention-hungry rebel leader?

To begin to understand the intricacies of Jesus' life – what He believed, and the way He moved about among the people, spoke out, and acted – which give us insight into how we should live our own lives as His followers, we must look at Rome.

As Richard Horsley so eloquently put it in his book, *Jesus and Empire*, "Trying to understand Jesus' speech and action without knowing how Roman imperialism determined the conditions of life in Galilee and Jerusalem would be like trying to understand Martin Luther King without knowing how slavery, reconstruction, and

9   Mark 10:45 (NIV).
10   Matthew 6:10 (NIV).

segregation determined the lives of African Americans in the United States."[11] It was the Roman empire that single-handedly determined the conditions of life in Israel when Jesus lived and inaugurated His mission. He lived in and under the rule of this society. And without knowledge of what life was like under the rule of the empire, we cannot see and interpret clearly what the God-man was really up to during His earthly time in Israel.

Rome was the capital city of a vast empire, and is regarded as one of the birthplaces of Western civilization. People have inhabited Rome since the year 753 BC and it was the Roman empire that had risen to become the most powerful civilization in Jesus' day. Not only did Rome wield supreme power, but its ruler – the emperor – was viewed as God on earth.

Rome expanded its territories and its rule by the sword, burning villages, enslaving any able-bodied people who opposed it, and killing the infirm ones.[12] The Romans were the ones to be reckoned with by the time Jesus stepped onto the scene, and as part of their quest for world domination it was not uncommon to hear stories of the complete annihilation (in the most extreme case) of cities under their rule.[13] Polybius, the Greek historian who lived around 200–118 BC, is recorded as saying, "It seems to me that they

11 Richard A. Horsley, *Jesus and Empire: The Kingdom of God and the New World Disorder* (Kindle Locations 188–189), Kindle Edition.

12 Horsley, *Jesus and Empire* (Kindle Locations 206).

13 Horsley, *Jesus and Empire* (Kindle Locations 239).

do this for the sake of terror" when commenting on the methods used by the Romans to achieve their destructive dominance.[14] By the first century AD, Rome had enslaved millions, killed countless souls, and terrorized and oppressed so much land that the boundaries of its empire matched those of the known world. Rome was a true superpower.

Caesar Augustus is credited with finally bringing peace to the empire, by means of the *Pax Romana* (Latin for Roman Peace) in 27 BC, which lasted for about 200 years. Augustus ruled at the time of Christ's birth, and this is where we find the backdrop to the nativity story.

Augustus, originally called Octavian and adopted by Julius Caesar, was the one who rose to prominence at this time. He put an end to large-scale military conflict and the empire experienced relative peace for two centuries. With this came great pomp and power. Horsley comments, "Acclaimed throughout the empire as the 'Savior' who had brought 'Peace' to the whole world, Octavian took the name 'Augustus' ('Revered/Highly Honored') and 'restored the Republic.' In the process he also established his own effective rule as emperor."[15] In 42 BC, Julius Caesar was deified as "Divus Iulius" and Octavian (his adopted son) added the title "Divi Filius" to his name, which means "son of the deified one/god."[16] This title implied religious

14 *The Histories of Polybius*, Book 10.
15 Horsley, *Jesus and Empire* (Kindle Locations 276–277).
16 Henry Furneaux, *Tacitus: Cornelii Taciti Annalium Ab Excessu Divi Augusti Libri Introduction*, Oxford: Clarendon, 1884. I: 63–66.

status but was used as a propaganda tool to increase his political authority.

There is an inscription from the Provincial Assembly of Asia, dated 9 BC, that tells of the emperor and the creed that accompanied his "divine" honor and glory. It reads as follows:

> The most divine Caesar... we should consider equal to the Beginning of all things... for when everything was falling [into disorder] and tending toward dissolution, he restored it once more and gave to the whole world a new aura; Caesar... the common good Fortune of all... The beginning of life and vitality... All the cities unanimously adopt the birthday of the divine Caesar as the new beginning of the year... Whereas Providence, which has regulated our whole existence... has brought our life to the climax of perfection in giving to us [the emperor] Augustus, whom it [Providence] filled with strength for the welfare of men, and who being sent to us and our descendants as Savior, has put an end to war and has set all things in order; and [whereas,] having become [god] manifest (phaneis), Caesar has fulfilled all the hopes of earlier times ... in surpassing all the benefactors who preceded him ... and whereas, finally, the

birthday of the god [Augustus] has been for
the whole world the beginning of good news
(euangelion) concerning him [therefore let a new
era begin from his birth].[17]

Did you get that?

Caesar Augustus was viewed throughout the empire as the savior who had brought peace and prosperity to the known world. The beginning of all things and the one who brought life and vitality had set all things in order, fulfilling the longings and hopes of all mankind. He surpassed all others in glory and was the beginning of the good news, and now it was time for a new era. He was the "son of the god," and his birthday would be adopted as the new beginning of the year worldwide.

According to the Romans at this time, their savior and lord (Emperor Augustus) had announced his new world order and was inaugurating his empire across the lands. He was to be honored, he was to be worshiped, and to believe or trust in any other was treason and blasphemy. This message was "carved in stone, on monuments and in inscriptions, around the known world: 'Good news! We have an Emperor! Justice, Peace, Security, and Prosperity are ours forever! The son of God has become King of the world!'"[18]

17 Source: the inscription of the decree of the Provincial Assembly of Asia, OGIS 2, 458, quoted in Horsley, *Jesus and Empire* (Kindle Locations 318–324).
18 Tom Wright, *Simply Jesus*, p. 30.

For someone living in the first century when all of this was going on, it was of incredible value to be connected somehow to the emperor. If you could not rise to become one of his entourage of officials, then the next best thing was to be connected to him as a citizen of the empire.

In fact, in that period, class and status were the two most important factors governing society. If you were a citizen of the Roman empire, you belonged to the elite ruling class: you were connected to the emperor, the savior. And as a citizen of the empire you would receive protection, certain privileges, liberties, and a status that outsiders (i.e. everyone else in the world) did not have. You could make a will, sue people, marry, vote, travel, and enjoy numerous rights in an era when universal human rights did not exist.[19] Your citizenship of the empire guaranteed you many rights and privileges that all non-citizens – pilgrims, migrants, foreigners, slaves, and everyone else – did not and could not have. In fact, it was assumed by the empire that if you were a slave or an outsider (a non-citizen), you were a thief or a swindler, and that if asked a question you would not tell the truth.[20] To obtain citizenship of the empire, either you had to be born into a family of citizens, or (for a very small minority of the extremely wealthy) you could buy your way in – and everyone else was out of luck. Therefore, there were only

19 Rowan Williams, "Outsiders and Insiders," lecture podcast. Holy Week Lectures on St. Paul at Canterbury Cathedral, April 2–4, 2012.
20 Rowan Williams, "Outsiders and Insiders".

two types of people: citizens and everyone else.

Let's stop here and think about all this for a moment. If this short excursion into first-century Roman history has taught us anything, I would suggest it is this: to the people of that time, citizenship or the lack thereof was of extreme value and importance. And as it was so central to the way society operated, it was natural that citizenship should become a matter of security and identity. With all of the societal pressures surrounding this matter, if you were lucky enough to be a citizen of the empire, your identity and security would be completely bound up in that. If you were not, that would significantly influence how you and everyone else saw you. I know it is hard to think in these terms today, because our world operates primarily on equality and the acceptance of people with different nationalities, backgrounds, occupations, religions, and so forth, but if we could suspend our own reality and try to place ourselves in the shoes of those living during the time of the empire, what we would find is a society in which everything came down to citizenship. Are you or are you not a citizen? Who are you? Where do you come from? Whom do you worship?

I had a great-uncle who was very much into genealogy. You know, ancient family-tree stuff. You probably have one too; every family seems to have someone in it that really enjoys digging into the lives of those who have gone before. I guess it gives them a sense of belonging or ties them to their roots. As the old saying goes, "You will never know where you are going until you know where you have come from." In my family this is a big deal: well, more of a joke big deal than a for-real big deal, but nonetheless, our genealogy pops up as a topic of discussion quite often when we all get together for family holidays and trips. You see, there are two types of people in my immediate family: those who are descended from the passengers on the *Mayflower* and those who are not.

My parents discovered a while back that, on the Peabody side of their heritage, there was a man who left England (London, actually) aboard the *Mayflower* – the famous vessel that transported 102 English Pilgrims to New England in 1620.[21] This means that some of our family are members of a prestigious society in America, the General Society of Mayflower Descendants, or, more commonly, the Mayflower Society. You might be impressed by this, but, trust me, you shouldn't be. All it means is that you have the ability to pay dues to the society and then take a tour of their museum. But when our family gets together, this is one of the jokes that will inevitably come up.

The story goes like this: my parents were on a trip in the northeast of America and drove over to Plymouth, Massachusetts, home of the Mayflower House Museum, to see what all the fuss was about. As they tried to enter, a man out front refused access to my mother, but allowed my dad

21 Abiel Holmes, *American Annals of A Chronological History of America, Vol. 1*, Cambridge: Hilliard, 1805, p. 199.

to go in and take part in the festivities because he, though not my mother, was a direct blood descendant of one of the passengers on the *Mayflower*. So, as my dad perused the annals of history and enjoyed the privilege and honor that his elite blood bestowed, my mother sat out on the curb eating an ice-cream cone all by her lonesome. This story lives on in infamy in our household. And what makes it even better is that I have two brothers and a sister, all of whose spouses are making an alliance with my mother and my wife as outsiders to our prestigious society. My dad, the three boys, and my sister have the bragging rights on this one, so whenever the subject comes up we turn up our noses and offer them an ice-cream cone.[22]

There is something within all of us that desires to be connected to something bigger than our individual selves. We want to be part of something more than what we can accomplish on our own. We long to be noticed, to be listened to, to be known and understood, and our identity – the way in which we see ourselves – is affected by all of these things. This, along with other factors, is why I found myself in the middle of an identity crisis the first year we were in London. In this new city, there was no longer any group of people, any larger community, any roots of any kind, or any history that I had been personally involved with. I had left all of those

22 In doing some research on the *Mayflower* for this book, I found out that our ancestor aboard the ship was actually an indentured manservant to a wealthier Pilgrim. I don't think I will be sharing this anytime soon with the unclean line of our extended family...

in Texas. It didn't matter that I was a pastor in the States, that the year before I had had a loving family and community close by, or that I knew who I was a year ago. The hard reality that I was encountering daily was that this was not a year ago; this was now.

My wife is a brilliant listener and counselor and has been given a real gift of speaking truth with grace. She often channels God's grace to me, helping to guide me into His truth, even when I don't want to hear it. I can still hear her voice in my head gently reminding me that my identity is not dictated by my circumstances. That is to say, my identity could not and should not be molded by my present situation. She was right. How I felt in London that first year was not a commentary on who I was. Regardless of who knew me, whom I knew, what I did (and how I explained what I did to others), how I felt, how unimportant or important I thought I was, or what I was spending my time doing, Jesus was the firm foundation of everything that I was, and that was not going to change.

Back to the Roman empire, but now enter the apostle Paul.

Paul was both a Jew and a Roman citizen.[23] He described himself as a "Hebrew of Hebrews" and a Pharisee at that.[24] By the standards of the world at that time, Paul had plenty to brag about. His family were well-off inhabitants of Tarsus (a

23 Philippians 3:5; Acts 22:27–28.
24 Philippians 3:5.

capital city of a Roman province), and thus Paul was born a citizen of the Roman empire.[25] In addition to this, he received training in the Torah (Old Testament Law) from the Jewish teacher Gamaliel.[26] He quickly rose through the ranks of Judaism and used his authority to effectively lead a terrorist snatch squad before his dramatic conversion experience.[27] Paul detested the new followers of Jesus, or Christians, as they were later called, persecuting many of them by throwing them into prison or even sending them to their death.[28] But, on the road to Damascus, the supernatural intervened.[29] Saul (as he was called at the time, before God changed his name) experienced a radical transformation that changed him so much that he went from throwing Christians into prison to being put in prison himself for the gospel. History tells us that, after serving as a missionary across the Roman empire and having fourteen books of the New Testament attributed to him, Paul was martyred for his faith in Jesus.[30]

Here comes the controversial part, the part that got him killed. In an age when Caesar was to be worshiped as a god on earth and being a citizen of his empire conveyed ultimate status, Paul, a Roman citizen, under the direction of the Holy Spirit began writing things such as this: "But our

25 Acts 22:3.
26 Acts 22:3.
27 Rowan Williams, "Outsiders and Insiders".
28 Acts 11:26; Acts 22:4.
29 Acts 9.
30 Ignatius of Antioch, *Letter to the Ephesians*, Chapter XII.

citizenship is in heaven. And we eagerly await a Savior from there, the Lord Jesus Christ."[31] And also this: "For he [God] has rescued us from the dominion of darkness and brought us into the kingdom of the Son he loves, in whom we have redemption, the forgiveness of sins."[32] If you read the pages of the New Testament closely, Paul lays out a citizenship and an identity that is greater than Caesar's. The citizenship Paul speaks of, and ultimately died defending, is a citizenship that is eternal, a citizenship that far surpasses the boundaries and times of the empire. A citizenship that is not of this world. According to Paul, becoming a citizen of the Kingdom of heaven is the ultimate identity in which all other temporal identities take up residence.

Of course, when Paul speaks and writes of this Kingdom citizenship, he is building on the gospel foundation that Jesus has already made clear. The story of God revealed in the pages of Scripture is the narrative of God finally becoming King of the world. And when Jesus steps onto the scene in the form of a man, He is "announcing that something is happening which is changing the way the world is."[33] The world's rightful King has come to earth in Jesus, and He has inaugurated His Kingdom, which is completely different from anything the world has ever seen. The announcement

31 Philippians 3:20 (NIV).
32 Colossians 1:13–14 (NIV).
33 N. T. Wright article: http://www.patheos.com/Articles/Let-Gospels-Speak-Patton-Dodd-06-15-2012.html
For more info on this, read: *How God Became King* by N. T. Wright.

Jesus was making is that "God's in charge now – and this is what it looks like."[34] Jesus' Kingdom, the Kingdom of God, or the Kingdom of heaven, refers to the reign and rule of the Father that was inaugurated in Jesus and will be completely realized once God triumphs over Satan once and for all.

But in the meantime, as we (the church) live between Jesus' first coming to earth and His next, we live primarily not as Brits or Americans or Australians, but as citizens of the Kingdom of God. This is our new identity, the identity that supersedes all others as the ultimate reality of our existence. It is through this lens that we learn to see our lives and the world in which we live. No longer are followers of Jesus defined by what we do, how we feel, where we live, what we spend our time doing, how much power (or lack thereof) we have, our socioeconomic status, or however else the world chooses to categorize us. But, rather, we are defined by being connected to the King of the universe. The moment we trust in Jesus and through faith turn to Him and He becomes the Lord and Savior of our life, we are transferred from the kingdom of this world to the Kingdom of God. It is this identity found in Jesus that will then be the center, the source, and the end of all that we are.

What Paul is saying here is that, in Jesus, "there is something you can belong to in which all other statuses are completely immaterial… where everyone stands on

34 Tom Wright, *Simply Jesus*, p. 61.

the same level."[35] It's like my dad coming to Christmas dinner and announcing, "Everyone is now a member of the Mayflower Society!" All are welcome, not just the elite ruling class or the rich who can buy their way in. Salvation in Jesus is open to everyone and citizenship in the Kingdom can be obtained by all. This was blasphemy to the empire then, and it's anathema in our world today.

No wonder the early church members were persecuted and killed. If a people who are under the subjection of the emperor start declaring allegiance to someone other than that emperor, and inviting others to do the same, they are going to come to blows. And that's what happened. Nero, who reigned at the time of the great fire of Rome in AD 64 (which he blamed on the Christians), was the first leader of Rome recorded as having extensively tortured and executed Christians.[36] But the empire did not have the last word. Jesus' death and resurrection had become the turning point in history; as recorded in Acts and Paul's letters, the resurrection people were convinced that history did not run through Rome but through the cross. They took Jesus' message all over the empire and the known world. For their identity was not that of a subject people under a worldly force, but a Kingdom people who were altogether otherworldly.

35 Rowan Williams, "Outsiders and Insiders".
36 Tertullian, *Apologeticum*, lost text quoted in [3], Eusebius, *Ecclesiastical History*, II.25.4.

These Kingdom people have been preserved throughout the centuries. From the time of Jesus and the early church all the way through history until now, God has been calling, redeeming, and claiming individuals for Himself and His Kingdom. This new birth gives Jesus' followers a new identity, not only as privileged citizens, but also as members of the royal ruling family. No longer are you Jill, who is a waitress and struggles with self-confidence. Instead, through Jesus, you are Princess Jill – the daughter of the King. No longer are you George, the hard-working student, whose dad never expressed love to you. Now you are Prince George – whose Heavenly Father's love is expressed so extravagantly that he has wrapped you in royalty, and is giving you a second chance. Wherever you find yourself today, right now as you are reading this, you need to hear that, in Jesus, you are a righteous son or daughter of the King of the universe – a prince or princess. This is real. This is true. This is your ultimate identity. And once you begin claiming this as your identity, you will be amazed at the clarity and freedom that you will find in living it out. Solid identity breeds security. Confidence in who you are allows for room to love well. Knowing whose you are gives insight into how you are to live.

In the C. S. Lewis classic *The Lion, the Witch and the Wardrobe,* there is a line spoken by the Beaver who is guiding the children (Peter, Edmund, and Susan) through their adventure in Narnia. He says, "They say Aslan is on the move – perhaps he has already landed." And then a very curious thing happens. The children all feel something quite different once the Beaver has spoken these words. "At the name of Aslan each one of the children felt something jump in its inside."[37] As the book unfolds you begin to observe that Aslan (who is God) refers to the children as kings, queens, princes, and princesses. Their encounter with Aslan has turned them into royalty, and is also showing them more and more clearly who they really are. The more they journey with him, the more they realize who he is and who they are in relation to him. Similarly, our encounter with Jesus makes us citizens of His Kingdom and a part of His royal family, and by pressing into this identity, we further realize who we are in this world because of Him.

37   C. S. Lewis, *The Lion, the Witch and the Wardrobe* copyright © C.S. Lewis Pte. Ltd. 1950. (This edition from *The Essential C. S. Lewis*, Touchstone, 1996, Chapter VII, pp. 88–89). Reprinted by permission..

2

Citizens, Colonies, and Communities

"The church is a colony, an island of one culture in the middle of another. In baptism our citizenship is transferred from one dominion to another, and we become, in whatever culture we find ourselves, resident aliens."[38]

Hauerwas and Willimon

"No one person can fulfill all your needs. But the community can truly hold you. The community can let you experience the fact that, beyond your anguish, there are human hands that hold you and show you God's love."[39]

Henri Nouwen

38 Stanley Hauerwas and William H. Willimon, *Resident Aliens*, iBooks, p. 18.
39 Henri Nouwen, *The Inner Voice of Love*.

Down by two, thirty seconds left on the clock as the visiting team, the Stallions of North Mesquite High School, come onto the floor hoping to pull out a come-from-behind win against the incredibly talented Carter Cowboys. Carter had three guys on the team that year who were moving on to play for a Division 1 university team, one of whom is now playing in the NBA. As we came out of the timeout and back onto the floor for the deciding moments of the game, we matched up, and, as it had been for the entire game, my assignment was to defend against Mr. Future NBA. This guy had run me all over the court for forty-seven minutes and thirty seconds. I was gasping for air, covered in sweat, with no more left in the tank; the whistle blew to see how this one would turn out. I was completely out of my league. The ball came out of bounds, and I don't really remember much else, other than passing it to our best player, who was in the corner, setup and ready to shoot the three. Dribbling around looking for an opening, our eyes met, I threw the ball, he sank the shot, the clock went to zero, and the twenty-five people (out of 600 in the crowd) who were in the away seats rooting for our team went absolutely wild. We had won by one point!

This wasn't supposed to happen. Carter was ranked very high in the state basketball polls that year and we were struggling even to win a few games. As we celebrated on the court while the home team and crowd just stood there shocked, we were quickly ushered by a group of police officers to our locker room to towel off and get changed before heading home. This wasn't the normal way of doing things after a big win. In the past, we had been allowed to celebrate on the floor, interact with our family and fans, and then leave the court of our own accord, with pride. But tonight we were in a hostile environment, on their home court, and we had ruined their record with this unexpected win. We changed out of our team uniforms into our street clothes, and once everyone had packed up, our coach was informed that our "police escort" was ready for us. You could hear them outside waiting. And by "them," I am referring to the enemy – the opposition, their team, and their fans. These people were intense. You could tell they weren't used to losing. So there we were, a group of sixteen-to-eighteen-year-old guys, fresh from our glorious win, petrified and huddled up together, with the police surrounding us to help make our way to the team bus. It was quite a sight.

I had never experienced anything like this before at a high school sporting event. People were shouting, spitting, threatening to knife us, using all sorts of name-calling and profanity... and those were just the mothers of the team. We finally reached the bus, loaded up, and then quickly sped off while people were striking the bus and continuing to yell as we departed. We got back to our side of town that night victorious and swelling with pride. We had gone into enemy territory, battled for a win, and then left chaos in our wake.

We celebrated, gave each other high fives, and vowed to not let anyone know that every single one of us was terrified in that locker room waiting for our escort.

I didn't realize it at the time, but our team on that night moved from being a group of individuals to a unified community. This shared experience brought us closer. We had faced a challenge together, fought, persevered, and come out on the other side different. Amidst the noise of the crowd that evening we knew whom we could trust, who was there for us, and who would meet us in the trenches.

I imagine the early Christians felt like this, although in a much more profound sense. Far beyond sport, the first-century followers of Jesus had experienced and were going through something that identified them as wholly "other." These individuals were no longer seen as people of the empire or part of the Jewish nation, but were rather now identified by their leader and themselves as people of the Kingdom. In direct opposition to the empire of the day, they were now in the thick of it. Whom could they trust? Whom could they turn to? Who was on their side?

Their answer was one another.

When the apostle Paul states that, through Jesus, "our commonwealth is [now] in heaven,"[40] he uses a Greek word, *politeuma*, which translates more succinctly as, "We are a colony of heaven."[41] And one of the dictionary definitions of

40 Philippians 3:20 (RSV).
41 Hauerwas and Willimon, *Resident Aliens*, p. 17.

a colony is a "beachhead, an outpost, an island of one culture in the middle of another."[42] Colonies are places whose inhabitants value the same things, live for the same cause, pass on these values to their children, and live differently and distinctly from the surrounding cultures. In fact, as some missional theologians have said, colonies consist of "resident aliens," who by definition live in a location in a land but nonetheless remain foreign to the greater majority. That night at Carter, our team were aliens. According to the locals, and affirmed by us, we didn't belong.

What I find most interesting about the colony of heaven in the Roman-occupied lands in the first century is that it pulled individuals out of the realm of Caesar and gave them residence in an international anti-imperial alternative. Jesus (and later Paul) was announcing that He (Jesus) was the true and better emperor of the world. No longer were these people placing their faith in their Roman overlord, but instead in the true emperor who had come onto the scene. And becoming a follower of Jesus wasn't just a personal decision that involved individual people, but a movement that was taking shape and bringing these individuals into a new colony. This alternative "Jesus movement" was radical. New citizens of the Kingdom were encouraged to find others locally and to live in real community with them. They were told to not compete with one another or to take advantage of others in

42 Hauerwas and Willimon, *Resident Aliens*, p. 17.

order to benefit themselves, but instead to love, sacrifice, and respect. This early community of Kingdom citizens lived in close proximity to one another, shared everything, and made sure that no one went without. They lived as brothers and sisters even when their earthly family lines indicated that this was not the case.[43] There was an ease in this new community that was so unlike the alternative society of the empire. These new citizens gathered locally, but also became part of a much larger global community. What had started in Jerusalem with the first citizens of this newly founded Jesus community spread, with local expressions beginning to pop up all over the empire. These localized colonies then spread throughout the known world, throughout history, and into our world today. The church, as we most commonly refer to it now, is the citizens' assembly, and our membership of it goes beyond mere belonging to being Kingdom royalty, with all the relationships and privileges that go with that status.

In the Roman empire in the first century, there was a tradition – carried over from the Greeks – of *ecclesia*, which was Greek for "the citizens' assembly." This was the meeting in each town or city that only Roman citizens could attend. At this assembly, citizens of the empire would gather to vote, hear appeals in open court, and take part in exclusive meetings of the specially privileged. Foreigners, slaves, and other non-citizens were definitely not welcome.[44] This was

43 Acts 2:42–47.
44 Rowan Williams, "Outsiders and Insiders".

one of the special privileges we mentioned earlier: status ruled, and if you were not a Roman citizen, you were left out. The first-century Christians living for the alternative Kingdom of Jesus quickly adopted the word *ecclesia* and redefined its meaning. Through Jesus, societal barriers had been broken down. The Roman *ecclesia* was only for the rich and privileged, but now, because of Jesus, there was an even greater assembly, the doors to which were thrown wide open to invite anyone in through Him. This Christian *ecclesia* soon became known as "the town meeting to which everyone can go."[45] In it, the idea of citizenship and belonging was turned completely on its head. Jesus' followers, the resurrection people, were living as citizens of an altogether different kind of kingdom – God's Kingdom. And in this kind of kingdom everyone was welcome at the party. It was open to all – slaves, women, foreigners, outcasts, the unclean, the imperfect, and even the self-righteous religious people… Jesus was the way in and the reason for the meeting.

As these early colonies of Kingdom citizens began taking shape, their goal was to live on earth as if they were in heaven. They had either encountered Jesus first-hand or been taught about Him by those who had. There was a movement of succession taking place, with those who had spent time with Jesus and learned from Him now passing all they had learned and observed on to the next generation, and so on.

45 Rowan Williams, "Outsiders and Insiders".

The way they strived to live together in these colonies was a direct result of an experience with Jesus... and I don't mean a physical one. It was the gospel that had transformed them and had saved them from sin and death. Separation from God had been dealt with by Jesus' death and these new faith-filled believers were crowned with a new citizenship in God's forever Kingdom. More than an individual salvation to escape the empire and hell, this salvation in Jesus united them all. They were not in this life alone. They were not on this new path by themselves. There were others, and if they were to live this new Kingdom way of life successfully, they needed each other.

Now there is a difference between knowing this truth and experiencing it. For a long time I knew in theory that this was the way in which God created us to live, but it wasn't until I experienced this communal way of life first-hand that I truly understood it. When I lived in Texas I created a fire pit. I use the word "created" because I was rather proud of this hole in my garden that I had dug out to hold a bonfire. There was something "cavemanish" about it that satisfied a deep testosterone craving within the founding members of the "Howl With Wolf Wang." Now I know this sounds like a reference to some sort of drug-crazed pack of Chinese wolves, but it's not – it is actually something much grander than that. Let me explain. The "Howl With Wolf Wang" (or "HWWW" for short) has gone through quite a few names over the years; "the Meeting of the Minds" and "High Council" were two of its predecessors. Less cryptic, this group consisted of two Matts, an Andrew, and a Rob, and further expanded to include our wives as we matured. Matt W., Matt L., Andrew, and I all worked and served in the same ministry in our early to mid-twenties. We all met at around the same time, or at least in the same season, and to this day I do not have any greater friends.

Matt L. and I were tasked with leading a colony (an island of one culture in the middle of another) of students and twenty-somethings in our city. Our dream and desire was to provide an authentic community for followers of Jesus in this age group. Our hope was that within this colony they would know others, be known, mature in their faith, become more like Jesus, and then be sent out to transform the place in which we lived. God's grace was poured out on us abundantly during this time, and these righteous desires were bearing fruit. Lives were being changed by Jesus and people's problematic pasts were being dealt with; wounds were healed, relationships formed, community realized… it was such a joy to witness. A year into our endeavor, Matt L. and I met Matt W. and Andrew. Andrew had just moved down from New York and Matt W. had recently moved into the city from the country. Socially and geographically, N.Y.C. and east Texas are about as different as it gets in the States, but, for all of us, it worked. These two joined Matt L. and me in leading the community, and what we experienced in those two years changed our lives forever.

We began "doing life" together, meeting up through the week, sharing meals, helping one another out, listening to one another, praying together, hurting for one another, and simply enjoying and laughing with one another. This was the beginning of a brotherhood. We had shared our experiences of working within the same organization, were committed to ministering alongside one another, and valued and learned to trust each other. Our common task of leading a "citizen colony" of twenty-somethings in Dallas brought us together, but it was our shared life that made us brothers. As we grew closer together, we were ushered into this unknown space that I had never been in before beyond my family – that of platonic brotherly love.

I remember commenting to Matt L. on one of my recent trips back to the States, as he was driving me to the airport to be dropped off, that my love for him made his wife dearer to me too: it made me care for her, and want to protect and serve her. Matt's wife, Lauren (who is one of my wife's very best friends), grew to be a dear friend to me as well, but there was something about the brotherhood that Matt and I shared that made me want to love the things he loved. There was a devotion blossoming, and it felt right.

Remember that garden activity I mentioned a while back? "Howl With Wolf Wang" became the code name for our weekly meet-ups, which we decided to have at my fire pit. We started with speaking code during the day to indicate an evening rendezvous at the pit. If throughout the day any one of us in the office used a four-word sentence with each word consisting of four letters, while giving a specific look, we knew we were on for that night. That worked for about two weeks until Matt W. came up with the brilliantly idiotic "Howl With Wolf Wang," and we have never looked back. For three years we went on a weekly adventure together that, although much less frequent now, still occurs. These are my best friends, and it was not by accident that God brought us together.

C. S. Lewis put it so eloquently this way:

In friendship… we think we have chosen our peers. In reality, a few years' difference in the dates of our births, a few more miles between certain houses, the choice of one university instead of another… the accident of a topic being raised or not raised at a first meeting – any of these chances might have kept us apart. But, for a Christian, there are, strictly speaking, no chances. A secret Master of Ceremonies has been at work. Christ, who said to the disciples "Ye have not chosen me, but I have chosen you," can truly say to every group of Christian friends "You have not chosen one another but I have chosen you for one another." The Friendship is not a reward for

our discrimination and good taste in finding one
another out. It is the instrument by which God
reveals to each the beauties of all the others.[46]

Friendship and community reveal to us not only the beauty of others, but also ourselves. Without true friends and the vulnerability that is required to be known by another group of humans, one cannot actually know oneself. It is within community that we learn about ourselves in a way that a life of isolation can never allow. And it is very easy to live a life of self-protecting isolation even amidst countless numbers of supposed "friends" and hectic busyness. But this is not the way God created humans to live. We need each other, we need to know others and to be known, and through this we experience joy in earthly relationships in the way that God intended.

There is a pub that I frequent in our part of London, called The George. It was built as a hotel on the High Street in 1752, but now it just serves as our local. (By the way, if you are keeping track, that pub is older than America.) I have breakfast appointments at The George once or twice a week, and every time I go, I notice the same thing. There is a different culture in the pub before 11 a.m. I usually arrive between 8:30 and 9 a.m., and as I sit with whomever

46   C. S. Lewis, *The Four Loves*, copyright © C.S. Lewis Pte. Ltd. 1960. (This edition London: Fontana Books, 1973, p. 83). Reprinted by permission.

I am meeting, eating my full English breakfast, I am always aware that 90 percent of the time we are the only ones eating anything, and 100 percent of the time we are the only ones under sixty. The older men have a certain table they all always go to, where they read the papers and chat to one another about the previous night's football – all the while *drinking* their breakfast. I still can't figure out at what age it becomes socially acceptable to order two pints of dark beer for breakfast, return to the bar for another one or two, and then go home to take a nap before noon (though I have to admit that some days that sounds like a good plan). Are their lives sad? Awesome? Dependent? I often wonder what goes on with these guys outside the pub, but as I talk to them, it seems more and more as if their life *is* the pub. One might say that, for them, this is their community. This is where they are known. This is where they know others. To them, the pub is their colony. It is their *ecclesia*.

Now I wouldn't say this is the life that God intends for them, but what I would say is that they are filling a relational void in their lives in the best way that they are currently able or willing to. This is where they feel they belong. So, as I sit and eat my breakfast and talk about the things of Jesus, I look around and am burdened. Burdened because I have experienced more. Burdened because I don't want my life to come to this. Burdened because I know that these men were created for something beautiful.

People in the global East[47] have historically been viewed as basing their identities and communities on tribal groups. According to the culture of tribal life, it is impossible to distinguish oneself from the tribe. In the East, your tribe is your social group, your clan, your people, your society. From my all-too-brief interactions with people who have been part of a tribe or clan in Africa and the Middle East, what I understand is that they cannot distinguish themselves from the greater community. If you were to ask a tribe member, "Who are you?", their answer would be something like this: "I am Michael, son of Akur of the Abizi tribe in Mozambique." This guy's identity lies in where he comes from and in whom he is related to. These are the identifiers of his life. You see this all through the Scriptures. Of course you would, as it was written primarily in the Middle East in ancient times. So when you come across books such as Zechariah and they start out telling you who Zechariah is, it's not surprising to find this: "In the eighth month of Darius' second year, the word of the Lord came to the prophet Zechariah, son of Berechiah son of Iddo…"[48] Zechariah was Berechiah's son and Iddo's grandson, and they lived during the time when King Darius reigned. This Eastern way of thinking permeates everything about a person in that culture. Of course the West is continually taking over more and more

47 The global East includes the Far East, West Asia, the Middle East (also known as the Near East), Central Asia, North Asia (Siberia), and South Asia (mainly the countries on the Indian subcontinent and below).
48 Zechariah 1:1 (NET Bible™).

ground and influencing cultures across the planet by means of globalization. But speaking specifically about the Eastern world's attitude to individuality, we find that it either does not exist or looks drastically different to our Western eyes.

If we were to ask the same question of John, a guy who lives in London, we would hear a radically different answer. "Who are you?" "Well, I'm John. I'm a financial trader in Canary Wharf." Or, to go back to my identity crisis earlier on in chapter one: "Rob, who are you?" "I'm a pastor." What we are getting at here is the issue of individuality that is the backbone of the Western world, and I would argue that individualism is the greatest barrier to Jesus-centered community. John is more than a financial trader. I am more than a pastor. These may be roles that we fill, but they are not what defines us. In the West, we find a breakdown of community. This world does not operate according to clans and tribes, but according to the individual. "You are special." "You are someone." "Try harder; be the best you can be… the captain of your own destiny." These are our mantras.

The individual self reigns supreme, and life is all about effectively becoming your own god. When community breaks down and the individual becomes supreme, people retreat to the places in which they can be a god. This is the natural response of selfish fallen creatures. Seclude yourself in a small world that you control. Cut out all of the things in your life that you don't have control over, and add things to your life that you do. It may be friends, relationships, spouses, material items, your dreams and desires, or how you spend your time. If you can manipulate these pawns in your life to satisfy and serve your "fleshly" agenda, then you have effectively become your own emperor. Bernard Shaw's definition of hell was: "… where you must do what you want to do." Effectively, in this type of world where the sovereign self reigns supreme, you become your own tyrant… and tyrants don't have friends. Tyrants don't have a community because no one is their equal.

Think about it this way. The Western dream is to do something you love, get paid well for it, have influence, have a family, be liked, own cars and maybe a holiday home, be comfortable, and spend your time doing only what you want *when* you want. You may invite others in to share life with you, but only on your terms and according to your rules. And the way the world works in the West, if you try hard enough and are dealt the right cards, this dream is not too far from becoming reality. It can be achieved.

Unfortunately, the colony is not immune to this oppressive line of thought… and when followers of Jesus think and live according to the rules of the Western dream (empire thinking), it breaks God's heart. In chapter 4 of Luke's Gospel, Jesus is being tempted by Satan when he (the Devil) spreads out all the earthly kingdoms for Jesus to gaze upon at once. Satan then reminds Jesus that these earthly realms are now under his control, and that if Jesus worshiped him, he would give them over to Jesus. Of course, Jesus refuses and rebukes Satan, quoting Scripture and putting him in his proper place.[49] As I read this passage recently, I was reminded that it echoes our dilemma. Just like the temptation in this scenario, compromising the lifestyle of a citizen of heaven does not suit us. We were not made for it, and therefore it will never satisfy us. It's not about what we do or what drives us. Followers of Jesus have been supernaturally changed, and the ways of the world no longer have power over us.[50] So, to chase after individual Western dreams, like the rest of a society that is under the power of Satan, makes absolutely no sense for a citizen of the Jesus colony. Our aim has been changed and, even more important, we have been empowered to live this new Jesus way of life by God Himself – through the Holy Spirit. Earthly kingdoms should not entice Jesus people the way they do the rest of the world. But unfortunately, this is not always the case. More to come on this later.

The moment we met Jesus, an invitation was extended to us to live in and for the only Kingdom that will last. The Christian colony is the only community in this world that will also exist in the next. There is a much grander story happening all around us, and if we are settling into the role of leading man or woman in our own little play, we are really

49 Luke 4:5–7.
50 Romans 6:22–23.

missing out. We are compromised, and are living lives that are incomplete. Life in the alternative Jesus community has been explained this way:

> Christian community, life in the colony, is not primarily about togetherness. It is about the way of Jesus Christ with those whom he calls to himself. It is about disciplining our wants and needs in congruence with a true story, which gives us the resources to lead truthful lives. In living out the story together, togetherness happens, but only as a by-product of the main project of trying to be faithful to Jesus.[51]

This invitation to live lives of love among brothers and sisters, to be a people who make a difference in the lives of others, to serve and to sacrifice, is made possible only because we see something that cannot be seen without Jesus. A universe-altering shift occurred in the world when the true King was born in obscurity, and then died in infamy on two pieces of wood. A Kingdom alternative was presented and a new people created. These people have aligned themselves with the true and better King, and to live rightly in His alternative Kingdom we need one another.

51 Hauerwas and Willimon, *Resident Aliens*, p. 116.

3

Citizens from All Tribes

"Unity in essentials, liberty in non-essentials, charity in all things."[52]
An ancient proverb most famously used by Richard Baxter (1615–1691)

"There is nothing more serious than the sacrilege of schism because there is no just cause for severing the unity of the Church."[53]
St. Augustine (AD 400)

Cris was a new vicar (senior church leader) in the poorest borough of London, based in a primarily Muslim community in the East End. He and his wife, along with their two young children, had moved into the area to replant a church that

52 Leroy Garrett, *The Stone Campbell Movement,* College Press Publishing, USA, 1981, p. 33.
53 St. Augustine, *Treatise On Baptism Against the Donatists,* Bk 5, Ch. 1, AD 400.

was at its last gasp and was threatened with being purchased by Islamic leaders who wanted to turn it into a mosque. Cris came from the north of England, and had spent the last few years in the West End of London – quite a different environment from the inner-city East. Cris and I met through a mutual friend the year we moved to London, and we instantly hit it off. One day we were walking the streets of his community and Cris was informing me about the history of the area. On this guided tour of old East London, I heard stories of Jack the Ripper, mafia bosses, drug cartels, social housing, and the emergence of Islam in the flats and tower blocks of the community. We walked, talked, observed, and prayed, and I asked a lot of questions.

We got off at Mile End underground station and were walking the narrow streets between the tower blocks of social housing when I asked a question, the answer to which rocked the church bubble that I was still operating from and working through. I asked Cris how it worked with all the different churches in the area, and what the relationship was between the local Baptist, Methodist, Evangelical Free, and Church of England congregations that I had noticed as we walked past. What was the spiritual climate? How did the churches view one another? What type of person attended each one? Was it a culture of competition, camaraderie, or ignorance of what the other churches were up to nearby?

Cris thought about my questions as we wandered

through a predominantly Bangladeshi market, and then gave me a straightforward answer: "It's like this. We don't have the luxury of large numbers like you are used to in America. Followers of Jesus make up less than 2 percent of the population of this country, and in this community far less. So, in our eyes, either you are a follower of Jesus or you are not. We are on the same team. We have to be. As long as you agree to the basic orthodox doctrines of the faith, you are with us." The matter-of-fact way he rattled off his answer proved to me what I had already come to realize. I wasn't in Texas any longer.

I ended up serving as the unofficial teaching pastor at Cris' church, All Hallows Bow, for six months, during which they started a new evening service aimed at the young professionals in the community. This gave me the much-needed time to learn how to preach and communicate in the British culture. It was a winner for both of us, and an eye-opener that I know God used to shape and form my views on His Kingdom work.

You may not realize how big a deal it is that I, an ordained Baptist minister from the States, was invited in and asked to preach regularly in a Church of England (Anglican) church. Back home, there is no way this would have happened! Baptist ministers aren't invited to preach in Episcopal churches, or vice versa. They are too different. In their eyes, we haven't been trained correctly. "You don't fit into our system." "We disagree with your denominational views on X, Y, and Z." I know this is not just an American thing; I have seen this denominational exclusivity in every country I have had the privilege of visiting. But to Cris, his church, and the congregations nearby, it was not just tolerated but celebrated that they had an "Evangelical Baptist American" in their Anglican pulpit. Not only was the culture outside the church beginning to feel post-Christian, but the thinking of the citizens inside the Kingdom was beginning to seem a little post-denominational too.

I have no desire to lie to you and claim that I am some sort of expert when it comes to church history: I am not. But, that being said, I do remember sitting in a church history lecture in which the professor came to the topic of "The Great Schism" of AD 1054. According to historians and scholars, the church as a whole did not experience any major division until the eleventh century. From the time of the messiah's death and the formation of the church at Pentecost (see Acts chapter 2), for roughly a thousand years the colony of Kingdom citizens was more or less on the same page. The early church grew and expanded, taking the message and the love of the resurrected Jesus to the uttermost parts of the world. As it developed, doctrines were needed, a common way of interacting and communicating emerged, practices developed, heresies were combated, and confusion and misunderstanding certainly arose with the spread of the church into different languages, peoples, and nations, but all in all, for centuries, the bride was not seriously divided. That is until 1054, when it all came to a head with the Eastern and Western groups drifting apart and excommunicating each other in what came to be known as "The Great Schism." The division was caused by theological arguments, specifically relating to the *filioque* clause of the Nicene Creed and the role of the Pope in the management of the church. This split officially divided the people of God into Eastern and Western churches, and later, even better known, the effects of the sixteenth-century Protestant Reformation further split the Western branch into many of the denominations we know today.

Cris reminded me through his words and actions that, as followers of Jesus, we are on the same team. It makes no difference that I grew up a suburban kid from the evangelical "Bible Belt" of Texas and that he grew up in the Church of England in Yorkshire. What matters is that each of us has found Jesus, and our citizenship is now in heaven. We are now brothers, and we will spend an eternity together. Sure, the lenses we have been given by our culture, traditions, and upbringing will affect how we see and interpret certain aspects of God and His church. But our goal must be unity in the foundations of our faith, the core of what we believe, and if that is the case, all the minor disagreements should be left as just that: trivial squabbles.

I'm not arguing for some liberal, emergent, unitarian tolerance of all faiths within the church or for compromise on the orthodox doctrines of our faith, but what I am pointing out is that we often spend more time, energy, vigor, and effort arguing with those supposedly on the same team than we do looking outward to the real issues of life and death in a world under the dominion of Satan. We must get over ourselves. If Jesus is the King in the colony, our gaze should be on Him, and when it is, these issues of competition and infighting are dealt with by the fruit of the Spirit. Allowing the Spirit's leading in our lives leads to love and solidarity among siblings, not fear and dissension.

Before Jesus went through His passion and was humiliated and crucified, one of the last things He did was to pray for His followers, present and future. Hear His petition to the Father: "The goal is for all of them to become one heart and mind – Just as you, Father, are in me and I in you, So they might be one heart and mind with us. Then the world might believe that you, in fact, sent me."[54] In other words, the Roman empire (and the kingdoms of the world to come) will know that Jesus is not just a rebel leader but actually God, by the way that His followers are united, and by the way that they love one another. They will be distinct and different from the world, acting with one heart and one mind to signify that they are "otherworldly." They will think,

54 John 17:21–23 (*The Message*).

believe, and act as aliens in this present world, which will serve as proof to outsiders that Jesus was not a lunatic or a liar, but the true King. If the church were unified it would speak volumes to those outside. Who else operates this way? Something must be different about these Christians.

Our third day in our new country brought a visitor to our door who, with hindsight, was a complete gift of grace to my family and me. The doorbell rang, Medea and I looked at one another in shock because we did not know a soul in the East End, and then I opened the door to a man with whom I would end up having a deep friendship in the seasons to come. Paul was his name. It turned out that he was a local vicar, and just happened to have an American wife. He asked if he could come in, told me that he knew my friend and colleague Robert (the guy from the rooftop in Jerusalem), and then asked if we could have a cup of tea and a chat. "Here's the thing," I told him. "I'm not really sure how to make proper tea. Paul, you go for it." And with our proper English tea we sat in the lounge and conversed. Paul was brilliant. Trained at both Oxford and Cambridge, he supervised our borough for the Church of England and was also helping to lead an interdenominational network of churches across the UK.[55] We instantly hit it off, and the next Sunday I was sitting listening to his teaching at All Saints Woodford Wells. If pushed to define himself according to the terms of the

55 New Wine: http://new-wine.org

day, he would consider himself a progressive charismatic evangelical, but – more correctly – he is a Kingdom bringer.

Paul and I shared many ideas, dreams, and experiences, most notably when he sat down with me to explain all the things I can and can't say in England, including an exhaustive list of swearwords and slang that would get me into trouble over here. Who could have known that quoting almost anything Austin Powers said – even in my best posh accent – would earn me weird looks and end conversations abruptly, all the while reinforcing the stereotype of an American trying to speak like the British?! This guy knew. After all, I am constantly reminded by Londoners that we (Americans) are the ones who have butchered the language.

Paul assumed the role of my unlabeled "cultural guide." I have found that everyone needs one of those when entering a new society. What are the norms? What is it OK to say and not say? What did they mean when they said _____? Am I interpreting this right? This was a type of cultural discipleship that really helped me to fit in and contextualize my life and the message I was bringing with me to my new land.

Later in that first year I had a dream. This was not normal for me. I don't typically remember my dreams very well, and rarely do I have a clue what they mean. This particular night I was an alien (hang in there with me) and had just landed on a distant planet. The task that had been given to me was to conquer this foreign planet for my people and claim it as ours. In the dream, I looked around and had a moment of realization while driving my alien planet walker: "I would be a fool if I did not first search this planet for other aliens who could join me in this great task." I had no clue whether other like-minded aliens existed, but for some reason I felt compelled to first examine the lie of the land, to try to join forces with others if they existed, and then to take over the planet… The next thing I know, the kids are awake and I am stumbling down to the coffee pot. Weird, I know.

Unlike others in the past, this dream stuck with me. As I processed and prayed through it, I became convinced that it was not about sci-fi people in a distant galaxy but actually about an alien people in the community in which I lived. This dream was about mission and the church. The more I thought about it, the more God revealed to me that the dream was about the season in which He had placed me. It was about my mission and the way it was to be carried out.

I booked an appointment with Paul and went to his office. After I had told him about the dream I went on to say that the most arrogant, individualistic Western thing I could possibly do would be to show up in his country claiming that I had all the answers. To think that I held the golden key to revival in a post-Christian secular society merely because I was seminary-trained and had served in an American mega-church in the evangelical haven of Texas would be extreme foolishness. (I have seen this attitude before in missionaries, and am convinced that it smacks of anti-gospel pride.) I told Paul that if we believed the Spirit had been at work in these islands since at least AD 200,[56] then it was moving long before I showed up and would continue long after we had left. I didn't want to be a lone ranger, but a brother. To set it within my alien dream scenario, I had been sent to London on a mission – to make much of Jesus in this city – and it would be foolishness to try to do this on my own. Therefore, I told him, I wanted to join in with what the Spirit was already doing there, and to maximize whatever God had given me to aid the expansion of His Kingdom, by living and working in collaboration with the other Kingdom bringers in the city.

He agreed and off we went in unity, doing more for the Kingdom together than either one of us could have done on our own.

We noted earlier that in the Gospels, when Jesus is speaking about His Father's reign and rule in the world, He calls this "the Father's Kingdom," "the Kingdom of God," or "the Kingdom of heaven." With these terms, Jesus is describing what it looks like when God is in charge. And as we also saw earlier, this was in the context of and in direct contrast to the Roman empire. Could it be that by using this language, Jesus expressly wanted to help people see that the Kingdom was completely different from the rule they

56   A. W. Haddan and W. Stubbs, *Councils and Ecclesiastical Documents* (1871), i, pp. 3–4. But see W. H. C. Frend in *Christianity in Britain, 300–700*, ed. M. W. Barley and R. P. C. Hanson (1968), p. 37.

were currently subjected to? That the Kingdom was directly and radically opposed to the empire? Rome expanded by oppression and the sword; Jesus' reign through sacrifice and service. Rome used fear, pressure, and hate, while the Kingdom advances through love, peace, and togetherness. According to the rules of the empire, you advance by taking advantage of others and putting your needs above theirs. You climb the ladder by stepping on the unwilling backs of others. But, by God's grace, another Kingdom is now at work on our planet. The fullness of God dwells in Jesus, not in emperors. We are small parts of a meta-narrative that is going on in the universe, and by framing our story within God's much larger one, we learn to understand and see ourselves correctly and live our lives accordingly. We must learn to live in the framing story of God's work throughout redemptive history, not the story of the empire.

Part of setting our individual stories within the framework of God's story means looking around to see what God is up to, finding out where His Spirit is already at work, and then joining in. We join Him, not the other way around. And when we do, we enter into His plan and design as co-laborers for the Kingdom. Not only co-laborers with God in His work, but also co-laborers with one another.[57] Which leads us back to the colony...

Follower of Jesus, you are an alien. I am an alien. We

57   1 Corinthians 3:1–9.

are aliens living as residents in our temporary homes and countries. This world is not your true home. When you encounter another alien, you are, in fact, rendezvousing with another conspirator who is a part of the greatest operation that this galaxy has seen and ever will see. There is only one being who is fueling and giving life to all of us aliens – the Holy Spirit – and we all have this in common. There is a unity in the Spirit, which is to be maintained by a bond of peace: "There is one body and one Spirit, just as you too were called to the one hope of your calling, one Lord, one faith, one baptism, one God and Father of all, who is over all and through all and in all."[58] Plainly stated, we are related not only to God, but to one another. We are all connected, and a passion for Jesus' gospel should lead us into a passion for one another – for the unity of His bride.

It took me thirty years to figure this out.

I am a naturally competitive person. In one of my previous church jobs I had to take a personality assessment that worked out my top five strengths, and competitiveness came out as one of them. In the sporting and academic fields this came in handy, and I would often harness it to help me to achieve the results I was after. This drive, this will to outdo others, came with me into the pastorate. It was a part of me, and for a long time I embraced it as such and would use it to fuel myself to work harder and try to outperform other

58 Ephesians 4:3–6 (NET Bible™).

ministers, churches, lay leaders, whomever. Of course, I never thought of it that way. It was always in the guise of "do all things as if you are working for the Lord."[59] So whatever I was doing, I would give it my all, give it my best, with what I thought was a healthy motivation, but in hindsight it was many times done in an effort to outshine somebody else. That's the thing about competitiveness: it is typically not directed inward but outward, in an effort to outdo others. What I came to realize is that with my covert competitive spirit within the church, I was killing unity. Competition is the arch rival of unity and has no business among siblings called to love and build up one another.

For those of you who are not church leaders, here is what tends to happen. Churches are led by humans, and humans are fallen individuals (this side of glory). Jesus has redeemed them, and the Spirit has taken on the business of transforming them to look more and more like Jesus. But the Christian journey also involves an effort of will. We work with God with our hearts open to His Spirit's leading, but Christlikeness does not strictly occur by osmosis. There needs to be a willful submission to the ways of God, and the more we practice this, the easier and more natural it gets. Your pastor is (I trust!) a godly person with a heart tuned to God, a calling, and supernatural gifts, skills, and abilities. But nonetheless he or she still struggles with the

59 Colossians 3:23.

flesh. That depraved nature within all of us, to which the Spirit will always be in opposition, will unfortunately, at times, rise up and crave fulfillment. And one of the ways in which this sin struggle bubbles up among people whose work and priority is the church is through competition with other churches, leaders, denominations, or networks. We (professional Christians) can get so caught up in trying to reach more and more people for Jesus (which usually comes from a good motive) that, in our efforts, we lose focus. The rationale behind reaching more people for Jesus gets blurred when that reaching requires more money, bigger buildings, greater programs, more "success" and wider influence. Again, these things are not all bad in themselves. But when we (professional Christians) begin referring to other churches as the competition, we have an empire problem. Of course, we never say it in public. We encourage and say the right things there, but behind closed doors (or the doors of our heart) we compete, we strive, we compare, and consequently we dishonor Jesus and His bride. Pride and egotism among the leadership of the church have no business in the Kingdom of God.

So far we have taken a glimpse into my life and the struggle for those of us in full-time vocational ministry, but to be honest, we all have these tendencies. We see it in our Bible studies, our home groups, the women's ministry, and the worship team, with the youth workers, and in our personal relationships. Something does not feel right to us when someone we are compared with gets more credit or attention than we do. It shouldn't matter, but it does. We know the right answer to why it shouldn't, but obedience to what we know is a completely different beast. Telling someone to love and actively doing it are two different things. I want to suggest that a lack of unity among the citizens in the colony is an obedience issue.

I firmly believe that if we want to see revival and transformation in our cities in the name and power of Jesus, then confession and repentance of competitiveness between brothers and sisters must occur. We have to get past this argumentative, judgmental, and prideful competitive spirit before we can live in love and unity even within our own family. There will be no denominations or brands of Christianity in heaven. They didn't exist in the early church either. Part of the Kingdom breaking through on earth as it is in heaven involves a dismantling of the system of the world and its reconstruction as a Kingdom society. The body of Christ is called and empowered to operate as this Kingdom society on earth, and this most definitely includes the way we do church.

What if we were truly and genuinely happy about the impact another believer was making for Jesus? What if we prayed for that person? What if impact for Jesus and His Kingdom were the evaluative measure for success in our communities and cities, not just in our individual Christian empires?

If we were to yield to the Spirit and obediently choose to love and engage with other believers in our communities and cities, the church would be an unstoppable force. Its life would resemble the stories told about the early church in the book of Acts: one heart, one mind, one Lord and Savior working in and through us.[60] A beautiful living picture that those on the outside could view and learn from that Jesus and His Kingdom are the ultimate reality.

60 Acts 4:32.

4

Citizens, Risk, and the Status Quo

"Twenty years from now you will be more disappointed by the things you didn't do than by the ones you did. So throw off the bowlines. Sail away from the safe harbor. Catch the trade winds in your sails. Explore. Dream. Discover."
Mark Twain

"Christ calls us to take risks for kingdom purposes. Almost every message of... consumerism says the opposite: Maximize comfort and security – now, not in heaven. Christ does not join that chorus."
John Piper[61]

61 http://www.desiringgod.org/articles/a-call-for-christian-risk

India, 1907

E. Stanley Jones was an American theologian from Baltimore, Maryland, who was born before the turn of the last century. As a faculty member at Asbury College, Jones felt called to missionary service among the outcasts of India, and in 1907 moved to his new land. During Jones' long ministry in India, he became close to Mohandas Gandhi, better known as the Mahatma. Their friendship greatly influenced both men, and many conversations were had, which Jones later recorded in his book, *Gandhi: Portrayal of a Friend.* Jones was the recipient of the famous Gandhi quote, "I do not reject your Christ. I love your Christ. It is just that so many of you Christians are so unlike your Christ."[62] Gandhi and Jones dialogued heavily about non-violence and peace, and later in his life Jones was nominated for the Nobel Peace Prize for his reconciliation work in Asia and Africa, and between Japan and the United States.

On one occasion, Jones approached the Mahatma and asked him, "How can we make Christianity naturalized in India so that it shall no longer be a foreign thing identified with a foreign people and a foreign government, but a part of the national life of India and contributing its power to India's uplift?" Gandhi responded with great clarity,

> I would suggest first of all that all of you
> Christians, missionaries and all, begin to live

62　E. Stanley Jones, *Gandhi: Portrayal of a Friend,* Abingdon Press, 1993, new edition.

more like Jesus Christ. Second, practice your
religion without adulterating or toning it
down. Third, emphasize love and make it your
working force, for love is central in Christianity.
Fourth, study the non-Christian religions more
sympathetically to find the good that is in them,
so that you might have a more sympathetic
approach to the people.[63]

The history books tell us that Mahatma Gandhi remained
a devout Hindu for his entire life and was assassinated by a
disaffected Hindu in 1948. As I read this quote from Gandhi,
something in my soul stirs. He was proposing that Christians
begin living more like Jesus, that Christians live fully for
Jesus without toning down or adulterating His message, and
that we emphasize love. Gandhi's perspective was that of an
outsider, and he hit the nail on the head.

The thing about being an outsider is that it gives you
a perspective that the insiders are not capable of obtaining.
Insiders may believe that they can think "outside of the box,"
but the very fact that a box exists, and they are the ones in
it, makes thinking from outside of it an arduous and nigh-
on impossible task. I am not Gandhi. I am far from sharing
his intellectual and philosophical brilliance, but I am an
outsider. We all are in some ways in our lives. A husband is
always an outsider when it comes to understanding the ways

63 Stanley Jones, *Gandhi: Portrayal of a Friend.*

of women, most visibly observed in his wife. He is close to her. He lives with her. He can be best friends with her, but he will never be a woman and see things completely from her perspective. As for me, I live as an American in the UK, which now makes me an outsider in two different nations. Medea and I joke that we no longer have a home, or at least it often feels that way. No matter how long I reside in London and how many of its customs I pick up along the way – the vocabulary, the ideas, the way I dress, how I approach life – at the end of the day, I am still an outsider. I didn't grow up here. I don't have a British passport. Therefore, I naturally see things from an outsider's perspective. What makes it even more confusing is that now I have left my homeland, I see that through a different lens as well: that of someone who has left and now lives in Europe. We all live in bubbles or pockets of society, and when I left mine to move to the UK, it brought with it a fresh set of insights into the bubble from which I had come.

The beauty and pain of not having a home is that it leads me to long for home, true home. A home with God, the way I was created to live. Many of us know or have experienced elements of this. When our earthly homeland is no longer where we reside, and we assimilate into another nation, we come to realize that "home" has more to do with identity and eschatology than it does with country of origin. Home is whom I am connected to, where I am accepted and valued.

For the believer, home is with God and His people. When no earthly nation is "home" on this planet, it causes us to long for the Kingdom, our true home, and the place where we can begin living now and will eventually spend eternity. For the Kingdom is what we have been adopted into as children of God. This is now what is right for our life. No longer are we storing up treasures and living for this life alone, but instead we are now living in light of the life to come. We take part now in Kingdom living that serves as a glimpse of the home we will have forever in the new heaven and earth.

One of the first things I noticed in London that was completely foreign to me was that there is absolutely no social pressure to be at church on a Sunday morning. Coming from the Bible Belt, where there was a real and noticeable divide in society based on where you were on Sundays, to a society that no longer experiences this cultural pressure was an eye-opener. In this city, Sunday is no longer defined by church; therefore, if someone is going out of their way to worship God, statistically speaking they are probably doing it for the right reason. I find this very refreshing. What this means specifically is that when you meet a follower of Jesus in London, they are a legitimate follower. I am living in post-Christendom where it is no longer assumed that one is a Christian. However, in my old life (although it's now beginning to wane), many very visible elements of Christendom were still knitted into everyday life.

My musings on this question of home and belonging, both earthly and spiritual, have thus led me to the conclusion that regardless of where you live, whether it be in the isolation of the outback of Australia, in a tenth-floor flat in Manhattan, at the epicentre of the Bible Belt, or in a majority Islamic community in West London, this statement remains true: citizens of the Kingdom should be the most risk-taking people on the planet. We have nothing to lose. Our present and future "home," found in Jesus, is the ultimate reality that His followers now live in. Our eternity is secure. We know where we are headed, which in turn should free us to live as people who take risks as the Kingdom bringers in our temporary and earthly homes. It does not matter whether our city or community is littered with church buildings or not; what matters is that, as well as being citizens, we have been reconciled, adopted, and given an inheritance as royalty in relationship with the true King, and he is sending us out to make a difference. It's like what Gandhi said about the Christians he saw: stop toning down your faith; stop compromising. Don't you know who you are?

I did a quick study recently on life expectancy in the United Kingdom and the United States and found that the average number of years that one can expect on this planet is eighty years in the UK and seventy-eight in the USA.[64] This is of course assuming that you don't walk across the road

64   http://data.worldbank.org

later today and get hit by a car whose driver is not paying attention. Every breath we take and every year we live is a gift of grace. But even seventy-eight to eighty years, in the grand scheme of the universe and history, is a blip on the page. I hate to put a downer on things, but we don't get very long. It was the apostle James who said that life is "a vapor, that appears for a little time, and then vanishes away..." and that we have no clue what will happen even tomorrow.[65] I don't know my great-grandparents' full names or what they did. What that means is that in three generations, your direct offspring won't have a clue about who you were, what you did, or what kind of mark you made in life. That's scary. This life is temporary.

How do you waste a life? Logically speaking, the answer would be by living for and spending your time on things that don't match up with who you really are in Jesus. One could call this a false life. If you have come to the conclusion that your ultimate identity and reality are that you are a citizen of the Kingdom of God, then not to live as a citizen would be living for something false, and living at less than your full potential.

Imagine what would happen if a member of the British royal family went around acting like a street sweeper... Prince William wakes up one morning and decides that the royal life does not suit him any longer. He can no longer be

65 James 4:14 (AKJV).

bothered: the responsibility, the demands, the always having to be "on show." He is fed up with it and wants a change. So he wakes up and tells Kate that he has had enough, and that he starts a new job today as a street sweeper outside of Westminster Abbey. Could you imagine the uproar this would create? The papers, the paparazzi, the royal family, the entire world would be watching him sweep the dirty streets via every media channel on the planet! The reaction to William and his brother, Harry, going to help the Army move sandbags to protect homes during the 2013–4 winter floods proves the point: they were met with a broadly positive response but also with an intense media presence. They cannot switch off from being royal. Even in going to help with flood-relief efforts, they were still recognized: they are who they are, and are therefore at the center of media attention, and they can't just decide they don't want to live like that any longer. The fact is, William was born the child of Princess Diana and Prince Charles. He is royalty… by birth. It is part of his identity, and so informs the way he lives.

Back to our earlier statement: citizens of the Kingdom should be the most risk-taking people on the planet. Why, you ask? Because we have absolutely nothing to lose. Citizen, this is your reality: you died with Jesus and were buried with Him.[66] You were united with Him in His death, and therefore you have already died, and there is no fear of death

66   Romans 6:3.

for people who have already died. Death has already been dealt with. What is the worst that can now happen to you? And beyond that, you were gloriously raised from the dead with Jesus so that you may live a new life.[67] Once you were brought from death (being dead and condemned in your sin) to life (forgiveness and freedom by and in Jesus) you were changed and are continually being changed to become more and more like Him. The Great Exchange occurred, and your sin and unrighteousness were placed on Jesus at the cross, and His grace and righteousness were lavishly poured upon you. You have been forever changed, and once you really realize this, you will be freed to live a life without fear. You will know who you are, whose you are, and where you are headed. And these truths are the only truths in the history of existence that can truly free you to live a life of taking risks. In this regard your identity as a citizen of heaven and as a royal child of the King shapes your choices and actions in all areas of life, even when that seems risky.

Why does God care so much about seeing His citizens take risks? Because Kingdom ground is not taken any other way. The life of the citizen is a life of living for the radical Kingdom of God. To live our lives as if the resurrection never took place is bowing to the idol of the false life. When we do this, we give in. We compromise, and we do not live for the true King and the only Kingdom that will truly last. Jesus

67   Romans 6:4.

is calling us to live with abandon for Him – to live in our communities in a manner that represents heaven on earth. And according to the world and wisdom of this age, this is radical. This lifestyle is risky, because living alternatively to the majority culture will cause you to stand out. It will require you to take a stand at times. It will make you uncomfortable, and often it will make other people uncomfortable around you. It is not safe, and it is not glamorous. But it is good.

You might be asking, why doesn't taking risks come naturally to me? Why is it so hard for me to step out and show my complete allegiance to King Jesus in lifestyle and action? If I could make a quick observation on this situation, I would say it is because we prefer other things. We prefer safety, comfort, routine, harmony, financial security, social status, even our family – all to the detriment of our relationship with Jesus. St. Augustine (the early church father who lived in the late fourth and early fifth centuries) put it this way: "Wherever you see fear, anxiety, worry in your heart… Follow those trails of smoke down to the fire of the altar of idolatry in your heart."[68] What Augustine means is that if we dig down deeply enough into the reasons for the things in our lives that cause us to worry, to fear, or to be anxious, we will find an idol that we are worshiping. An idol is anything in our lives that we hold dearer than Jesus or turn to for strength that is not Jesus.

68   St. Augustine, *Confessions*.

Idols come in all shapes and sizes, and are especially suited to each individual and the situation in which they find themselves. They can be good things, even great things... but when they replace God in our lives we go off balance. We end up bowing to the idols in our heart instead of to God, hoping these things will provide the end results for which we are looking. But they never satisfy. We don't take risks for the Kingdom because we prefer to call the shots and live for the false gods of our hearts. We serve those idols and soon enough they enslave us. I can't tell you how many Christians I have met who set out in their youth to provide a comfortable life for themselves and their loved ones, but realized later on that their entire life had been spent on achieving this goal. They had missed the point. They started off in a good way, hoping to provide safety and security for those they loved, but then looked back and discovered that the idol had got a grip on most aspects of their life. When we cling to something, we cannot open our hands to what the Father wants to give us.

I think we can look at it in light of another quote attributed to E. Stanley Jones: "We inoculate the world with a mild form of Christianity so that it will be immune to the real thing." What I believe Jones was getting at is this: in the West, we have a terrible reputation for proclaiming our allegiance to Jesus, going to church, and then fitting what we learn about Him into our lives whenever it is convenient. One minute we say we worship Jesus, and the next we show that we really worship everything else. Consequently, the watching world sees a lukewarm faith that doesn't translate from Sunday to the rest of the week. Jesus gets compartmentalized, and compartmentalization means He does not have free rein over all that we are. The outside world sees this, decides that, no matter what we say, Jesus doesn't really make all that much difference, and then goes about its business. They have been inoculated. They had a taste, and now they are immune when the real Jesus follower comes around.

Risk takers for the Kingdom break out beyond this. Risk takers are the people who find their security in Christ and rely on Him "and the shape of His Kingdom to give meaning and significance to their lives."[69] His story gives both framework and shape to their lives, and therefore living appropriately as a citizen of the Kingdom becomes regarded by the world (and often even by the church) as radical.

In London, the not-for-profit organization Awaken inspires, educates, and equips missional communities that are made up mostly of people in their twenties who come together to form a colony of believers desiring to live this Kingdom way of life in our society. We come together weekly to eat, pray, discuss, and study, and go out as a community with a mission to live out our faith as we interact with the outside world. Our goal is not a Bible study or fellowship

69 Hauerwas and Willimon, *Resident Aliens*, p. 133.

group where we all just become smarter Christians, but rather a community that lives for mission in the world in which we find ourselves. Everything we do is centered on becoming more like Jesus and then living like Him in a lost and broken world: with no compartmentalization. Compartments lead to Pharisaical living or secret lives.

I was informed recently that we have been labeled "radical" by other believers in the city. This is exactly my point. This is not radical, this is biblical. A thing should not be considered radical if it is what we are supposed to be doing in the first place. In fact, the word "radical" comes from the Latin *radicalis* or *radix,* which actually translates as "root."[70] And to be rooted in something is to find the basis of that something in its primary source. Therefore, to be radical in your faith would mean being rooted in your faith and in its founder, Jesus. The roots are in Jesus, and then the fruits that spring up (which may look radical to some) should be the natural and healthy outcome of being rooted in the first place. To put it another way, as the old saying goes: "The root bears the fruit."

I can understand Awaken being labeled as radical by those outside of the church – to them it probably is. But to the church, this should not be so. Taking risks for the Kingdom will cause us to be seen as radical by those living for the idols of security and comfort.

70   http://www.merriam-webster.com/dictionary/radix

Joshua and Caleb were risk takers. The Israelites had been freed from their captivity at the hands of the Egyptians and led out of Egypt by Moses in supernatural fashion: the waters of the Red Sea parted to allow God's people to escape, and then came crashing down on their oppressors. God had given His people freedom from captivity and bondage, and was now leading them to the Promised Land. This was the land that had been described as "flowing with milk and honey"; it was exceedingly good and the place that God had promised for His people.[71] They had made it … well, almost. As Moses and the people got closer to the land of Canaan, the Lord spoke to Moses and instructed him to send out twelve spies who would go and investigate their new homeland and report back to the nation before they moved in. Moses picked out twelve leaders who were up for the task and sent them out on this journey for forty days. Before they left, he told them to take notes on what the land was like, to observe it, to bring back some of its fruits, and lastly, to "be brave" as they set off on this adventure.[72]

The forty-day secret investigation of the land came to an end, and as the spies returned to report back to Moses, Aaron, and the community, things got interesting. They had seen the land. They saw that it was incredible and indeed "flowing with milk and honey." It had everything God had promised them; it was going to be an amazing

71 Numbers 14:8.
72 Numbers 13:20.

new home. However, there was a problem: their Promised Land was currently home to ferocious giants with fortified cities and an appetite for outsiders. This was in the spies' report. The inhabitants of the land were of great stature, and some of them – the Nephilim – were so huge that they made the Israelites look like grasshoppers, even to themselves.[73] The consensus was that Moses (and by extension God) would be crazy to send them into this land to be massacred by its current occupants who apparently totally outclassed them.

That was the overwhelming opinion of every one of the spies, except Caleb and Joshua. These two saw something different and were ready to take action. It's as if they saw it through a different lens from the others. As the other ten were giving all the reasons why Israel should not go into this land, Caleb silenced them and boldly said, "Let us go up at once and occupy it, for we are well able to overcome it."[74] The others persuaded the crowds with tales of woe and inadequacy, and at the end of this conversation the people refused to go into the land. In fact, they actually said ridiculous things like they "wished they had died back in Egypt... surely that would be better than this fate." They wept and proclaimed that slavery and bondage back in Egypt would be better than taking the risk of moving forward to what God had already promised them. If they

73 Numbers 13:33.
74 Numbers 13:30 (ESV).

didn't take this chance, they might not be happy, but at least they would be safe.

What followed shows the risk of *not* taking a risk. God intervened. He told His people that, because of their disbelief in Him, their lack of faith, their disobedience, and their trust in what they saw and not in what He had promised, they would all die in the wilderness.

All of them.

They would never inherit the land. This generation would die out, and their children would be the ones to enter the Promised Land. They were not willing to take the risk, and the consequence would be a lifetime of wandering – forty years to be precise. God told them: "… your dead bodies shall fall in this wilderness. And your children shall be shepherds in the wilderness forty years and shall suffer for your faithlessness."[75] The cost of being unwilling to take a risk was a life of wandering for everyone in the entire nation but Caleb and Joshua. Everyone would wander and then die except them. No one would *truly* live but these two, who saw the situation with eyes of faith and trusted God enough to put it all on the line. This is how it is recorded in the book of Numbers: "None of those who came up out of Egypt who are twenty years and older will ever get to see the land that I promised to Abraham, Isaac, and Jacob. They weren't interested in following me – their hearts weren't in it. None,

75 Numbers 14:32–33 (ESV).

except for Caleb son of Jephunneh the Kenizzite, and Joshua son of Nun; they followed me – their hearts were in it."[76]

What caused Caleb and Joshua to step out, do the unpopular thing, and decide to go against their entire nation and risk everything? I think we have just read the answer: they were characterized by God as people who had "wholly followed the Lord."[77] Here were two men who were willing to risk it all; two men who understood their identity and by faith were willing to claim what was promised. They were completely devoted to the Lord, and therefore saw things from His perspective and refused to trust their own limited viewpoint.

I imagine the early Christians living in the Roman empire might have felt the same way. Their leader (Jesus) had just been murdered and now they were left to live out and spread His gospel message as a newly founded colony amidst a godless land of oppression and idolatry. Neither the empire nor the Jews were in agreement with how they were now choosing to live. Caesar would probably have thought this would all fade once the soldiers had done away with the rebel cult leader, but instead the colony continued to strengthen and expand. The persecution increased, and the famous quote by Latin apologist Tertullian rang ever more true: "The oftener we are mown down by you [Rome], the more in number we grow [followers of Jesus];

76 Numbers 32:11–12 (*The Message*).
77 Numbers 32:11–12 (RSV).

the blood of Christians is seed."[78]

What if our first-century spiritual ancestors had not yielded to the Spirit and followed God's leading in the face of opposition and hardship? What if they had chosen safety instead of faithfulness? What if they had compromised their message in order to protect themselves and their loved ones? What if they had just wanted an easy life, and quite honestly could not be bothered? What if they had been unwilling to take a risk for the Kingdom? God is glorified by the fact that we did not have to find out.

What does taking a risk as a citizen of the Kingdom of God look like for you? Right now? In your situation? Where are you choosing to allow the idols of safety, security, comfort, or self-protection to provoke fear, anxiety, and worry in your heart? In what ways are you unwilling to step out and claim what King Jesus has already promised you?

It's time for you, citizen, to believe in who you are and allow that to change how you live.

78 Tertullian, "Apology," in *The Ante-Nicene Fathers*, Vol. 3, Alexander Roberts and James Donaldson, eds (Albany, Ore.: AGES Software, 1997), p. 102.

5

A Citizen's Allegiance

"Christianity, if false, is of no importance, and if true, of infinite importance. The only thing it cannot be is moderately important."[79]

C. S. Lewis

"For everything, absolutely everything, above and below, visible and invisible, rank after rank after rank of angels – *everything* got started in him and finds its purpose in him. He was there before any of it came into existence and holds it all together right up to this moment... He was supreme in the beginning and – leading the resurrection parade – he is supreme in the end... Not only that, but all the broken and dislocated pieces of the universe – people and

79   C. S. Lewis, *God in the Dock: Essays on Theology and Ethics*, copyright © C.S. Lewis Pte. Ltd. 1970. (This edition Harper Collins, 1970). Reprinted by permission.

things, animals and atoms – get properly fixed and fit together in vibrant harmonies, all because of his death, his blood that poured down from the cross."
Excerpt from Colossians 1:15–20 (*The Message*)

Last year I swore my allegiance to a British/Turkish Cypriot Muslim man wearing lycra in Epping Forest just outside of London.

Seref was covered in sweat, eating a protein bar, and standing over me with a grin like that of a child who has crept down early Christmas morning to sneak a peek at what Santa has brought before his parents wake up. No, Seref was not a cross-dressing jokester with a protein deficiency; he was my friend. And this friend was giving me a two-month tutorial on the art of European road cycling to get me up to speed before we embarked on the adventure of a lifetime that is the ride from London to Paris. For many cyclists in the United Kingdom, L2P (London to Paris) is the challenge that becomes the ultimate goal for the serious road rider. Imagine running three half marathons in three consecutive days, and you will begin to catch a glimpse of the amount of energy and subsequent exhaustion that this journey entails. In Texas, men get beaten up (or worse) for wearing lycra in public. In Europe, it is celebrated, especially in France where the national sport is cycling.

The day I pledged allegiance to Seref and his "wolf pack" of four Turkish Cypriot brothers, as they affectionately referred to themselves, was a turning point in my cycling career. I didn't see any other way. I had to do it. I was flat on my back on the ground in absolute exhaustion after my first fifteen-mile trial ride, while Seref stood over me with infectious zeal and an ambition to quickly mold me into a cyclist. His goal was to make this Texas boy wear lycra… and like it. That day, that moment, Seref became my cycling Yoda. I had got into the sport hesitantly, but from that point on there was no turning back. I was going to allow Seref to have his way with me and lead me until we basked in glory under the brilliant lights of the Eiffel Tower in Paris.

Seref and I had met through our wives, when they were taking our kids to the same weekly playgroup. We had a few dinners together, instantly connected, and from that point on, began to develop a friendship. My new friend had been born in London to Turkish Cypriot parents who practiced Islam. Consequently, he looked like a Turk but had a proper British accent and had been brought up with a mixture of Western ideologies and Islamic cultural beliefs. Seref was a leader, the alpha male of the brothers, with a sharp mind and a driven personality. We got along so well. Two guys from very different parts of the world with totally different backgrounds were getting to know one another and share stories, ideas, and beliefs which unbeknown to me at the time were leading me toward lycra.

One day, Seref and I met at our local pub after work

to hang out, and the conversation moved on to Jesus and religion. Seref knew full well who I was, what I believed, and what I did for a living … as far as he could understand it from his viewpoint. Anyway, we began to discuss the different major world religions and the differences between them. I was articulating to Seref the difference between Jesus and His gospel and all of the other faiths. We worked our way through Buddhism, Judaism, Hinduism, and Islam, and had just come to Jesus when he asked the most intriguing question: "So how does race fit into all of this? You know, because Jesus was a white American just like you."

"Whoa! Time out!" was my immediate response. "Say that again."

"What, everyone knows that Jesus is from America and looks like you."

After some quick historical explanation and a lesson on Middle East geography, I was able to explain that Jesus looked a lot more like him than he did like me. In fact, many of his family's cultural habits and ways of life probably had much more in common with the origins of the Bible in the Middle East than with the postmodern worldview of the West. One thing I value about Seref is that he is open-minded. He is willing to think as objectively as he can and weigh the arguments. This conversation at the Cuckfield pub somehow then took a turn and digressed into much more important matters, such as cycling.

Seref wanted me to go with him and his brothers on this cycling trip from Tower Bridge in London down to the White Cliffs of Dover, across the English Channel on a ferry to Calais, France, from Calais through the hills down to Amiens, and then victoriously into Paris. I had not ridden a bike since I was thirteen. But the chance to develop our friendship and the thrill of the challenge led Seref and me to Gumtree (an online garage sale) to find a road bike. Seref found me a bike, loaned me the necessary gear, and began teaching me the ropes. Each week he would send articles, emails, tips on nutrition and cycling fundamentals, and videos to watch online. I was undergoing a training regime and I had to get ready because we were leaving in two months.

The day came: we set off from Tower Bridge – I was still learning how to clip my shoes into my pedals that morning – and began our eighty-five mile ride to Dover. We cycled all day to Dover, all day the next day to Amiens, and all day on the third day to Paris. And when we pulled up next to the Eiffel Tower at 8 p.m. and collapsed beneath it in an untidy pile of bikes and men, we had conquered it! We were victorious. Tourists offered to take our pictures, we held our bikes above our heads, and then stayed up the entire night swapping stories and bonding like men who had just come through a battle. We had been through one crash in a small French village (where a farmer helped repair a broken bike), countless cramps and dehydration, mass consumption of rehydration drinks, energy bars, and gel packs, and when all was tallied we had each burned over 15,000 calories in our 290-mile trek to France's capital. It was the hardest, yet most exhilarating sporting experience of my life.

Allegiance is loyalty or commitment to an individual or group. It is synonymous with faithfulness, obedience, and devotion.[80] In a political context, having an allegiance to something or someone implies the duty of fidelity owed by a subject or citizen to their sovereign or ruler. Citizens pledge their allegiance to the supreme power in a nation. In the UK, the "Oath of Allegiance" was originally established as part of the Magna Carta of 1215 for rebels who were required to reaffirm their loyalty to King John;[81] this type of oath has been used through the ensuing centuries, and, in accordance with the Promissory Oaths Act of 1868, certain public servants and newly naturalized subjects still swear an oath to the Queen. It states: "I, *[insert full name]*, do swear that I will be faithful and bear true allegiance to Her Majesty Queen Elizabeth, her heirs and successors, according to law. So help me God."

In America it is much the same. Once they have qualified, citizens wishing to be naturalized in the United States of America go through a ceremony in which they swear an oath called the "United States Oath of Citizenship."

80 *Merriam-Webster's Collegiate Dictionary, 2004.*
81 *ENGLANDS OATHS. Taken by all men of Quallity in the Church and Common-wealth of ENGLAND*, published by G. F. London, printed in 1642.

It reads:

> I hereby declare, on oath, that I absolutely and
> entirely renounce and abjure all allegiance and
> fidelity to any foreign prince, potentate, state, or
> sovereignty of whom or which I have heretofore
> been a subject or citizen; that I will support and
> defend the Constitution and laws of the United
> States of America against all enemies, foreign
> and domestic; that I will bear true faith and
> allegiance to the same; that I will bear arms on
> behalf of the United States when required by the
> law; that I will perform noncombatant service
> in the Armed Forces of the United States when
> required by the law; that I will perform work
> of national importance under civilian direction
> when required by the law; and that I take this
> obligation freely without any mental reservation
> or purpose of evasion; so help me God.[82]

Throughout history, in both countries and in other nations around the globe, citizens, peoples, or republics have had some sort of pledge, song, or oath of allegiance by which they commit to being loyal to the sovereign or leaders of that nation. It was no different in the Roman empire. Every five years, each male citizen was obliged to register for

82 http://www.usimmigrationsupport.org/oath-of-allegiance.html

the Roman census and declare his "family, wife, children, slaves, and riches."[83] Registration for the census meant freedom. This was the only way that a "Roman could ensure that his identity and status as a citizen were recognized."[84] Registration made these citizens a part of the Republic, and failure to do it barred them from obtaining citizen status and the rights and privileges that accompanied it. There was also an allegiance to be sworn to Caesar. Below is an inscription translated from the original Latin from the year 3 BC:

> In the third year after the twelfth consulate of the emperor Augustus, the son of the divine Caesar, 6 March, at Gangra, in the marketplace: this oath was sworn by the Paphlagonians of the area and the Romans engaged in business among them.
>
> I swear to Zeus, Earth, Sun, all the gods and goddesses, and to Augustus himself, that I will be loyal to Caesar Augustus, his children, and descendants all through my life, both in word, deed, and thought, holding as friends those they hold as friends and considering those as enemies whom they judge to be such, that with regard to things that concern them I will not be sparing of my body or my soul or my life or children, but will face every peril with respect to

83 http://www.roman-empire.net/society/society.html
84 http://www.roman-empire.net/society/society.html

things that affect them. If there is anything that I should recognize or hear as spoken, plotted, or done contrary to this, I will report this and be an enemy of the person speaking, plotting, or doing any of these things. Whomever they judge to be enemies, I will pursue and defend against them by land and sea with arms and steel.

If I should do anything contrary to this oath or fail to follow up what I have sworn, I impose a curse upon myself encompassing the destruction and total extinction of my body, soul, life, children, my entire family, and everything essential down to every successor and every descendant of mine, and may neither earth nor sea receive the bodies of my family and descendants nor bear fruit for them.[85]

The last section of this oath of allegiance to Caesar Augustus is the most telling. To put it bluntly, if a person reciting this oath did anything contrary to what they had promised, a curse of the complete destruction and extinction of that person and their entire family would be put upon them. It would pass down to every descendant, and this fate was a potential outcome for them when vowing allegiance

85   Tim G. Parkin and Arthur J. Pomeroy, "Inscriptiones Latinae Selectae 8781" (Paphlagonia, 3 BCE), in *Roman Social History: A Sourcebook*, copyright © Tim G. Parkin & Arthur J. Pomeroy, 2007, Routledge, an imprint of the Taylor & Francis Group. Reprinted by permission.

to Caesar. An interesting point to note is that people did not swear allegiance to the Senate or the Roman state (or empire), but rather specifically to an individual, to Caesar Augustus. Loyalty was not to be given to Rome, but to Caesar. And as we have already mentioned, Augustus' divine status demanded complete loyalty and allegiance from his people. The lordship of Augustus gave him supreme control through his lands.

I'm glad I didn't make this kind of deal with Seref.

First-century Christians pledged allegiance to the Kingdom of God, and followers of Jesus do the same today. We don't swear allegiance to the modern equivalent of Caesar but to King Jesus and His Father's Kingdom. I realize these early Christians may have lived in the Roman empire and even been citizens of it, and we now are citizens of the countries in which we live. We all have multiple loyalties that we must balance in order to live in our society on this planet. However, as we are citizens of the Kingdom of God our allegiance to King Jesus must take precedence over every other commitment. More to come on this later.

For the first Christians all the way up to the most recent ones, when they found Jesus they entered into an ultimate allegiance. This is to the King who set them free and brought them into His life. The funny thing is, I don't think many of us today see it this way. Sure, Jesus died in our place, and has given us new life. He's there when we need Him or when we get into trouble, but we don't fully understand and may not be willing to commit to what He actually requires of us. We would rather take the good parts (the benefits) of a relationship with Jesus, and leave the heavy allegiance business to the monks and nuns. We do this with our other earthly commitments as well. It comes with being human. Part of the problem is that we don't have a proper view of ourselves.

Right now, I am writing this chapter while sitting out by a lake in a small town, surrounded by tall pine trees. They are everywhere. Imagine that you were in the furthest galaxy known in the ever-expanding universe and were given a super-high-powered cosmic camera that could zoom in a billion times. If you were to start zoomed in on my computer and then begin zooming out toward space you would see first my keyboard, then two hands, then a computer screen, then me, then some trees, then the tops of the trees, and you would probably then see the lake nearby. Keep zooming out and you would see the land surrounding the lake, then up into the clouds, then the lights in this small town, then further up you would see the country I am in, then earth, then the other planets, then the Milky Way, then the other galaxies, and finally back into your camera from the furthest point in known creation. From this viewpoint, I am just a speck in the cosmos, and so are you.

Congratulations, you are now appropriately small.

Unfortunately, for many of us, the improper perspective that we cling to by default because of our inherited sinful nature often turns our allegiances inward, where they become self-absorbed. We make a commitment and are loyal to ourselves and the things that we deem worthy of our love and fidelity. When given over to fallen human nature, which is in opposition to the Spirit, this is how we live. We are Caesar and we pledge allegiance to ourselves. This is our unstated heart position. And when we are the one with whom our allegiances lie, we become the sovereign of our own little isolated empire. St. Augustine of Hippo is believed to have been the first to use the Latin term *incurvatus in se*, which translates as "curved inward on oneself," as a way of describing this default heart position.[86] What he was saying is that the natural state of our sinful heart and soul is self-absorption and -protection. We are natural born navel gazers. Imagine bending at the waist and hugging your chest. This is the natural posture of our heart. We curl up into a protective position bent in on ourselves, and there is only one thing that can free us from this slavery: Jesus.

The true and ultimate King of the universe humbled Himself to die to set us free from a life of perpetual navel gazing.[87] In Jesus, our heads and hearts can be raised from self-centeredness to a position in which they are looking up to receive from and give worship to Him. In Jesus, the hands

86 Matt Jenson, *Gravity of Sin*, T. & T. Clark, 2006.
87 Philippians 2.

that grasp and cling to our idols can be released and opened to receive what He eagerly wants to give us. The true King wants to relieve us of the ever tiresome and worrying burden of operating as our own emperor. It is impossible to be truly fulfilled in this life when our allegiances lie with anyone or anything that is not King Jesus. It is how God has set the universe up.

Not only must we be freed from navel gazing, but we must also be freed from enslavement to the empires of "the world." As Bob Ekblad writes in his book *A New Christian Manifesto*, entering the Kingdom of God as one of God's beloved citizens of heaven "first necessitates departure from the 'world.'"[88] He goes on, "If we are to see God's Kingdom come and will be done, on earth as in heaven, we must first recognize that what we mostly experience here on earth is not heaven, and may actually feel closer to hell for some."[89] For those of us who have much vested in the benefits of the world, this truth becomes harder to see. It was Jesus who said, "Truly I say to you, it is hard for a rich man to enter the kingdom of heaven. Again I say to you, it is easier for a camel to go through the eye of a needle, than for a rich man to enter the kingdom of God."[90] In other words: to enter into God's Kingdom via trust in Jesus, we must first *leave behind* the empires and systems of this world. When the

88 Bob Ekblad, *A New Christian Manifesto: Pledging Allegiance to the Kingdom of God*, Westminster John Knox Press, p. 52.
89 Ekblad, *A New Christian Manifesto*, p. 52.
90 Matthew 19:23–24 (NASB).

Spirit indwells believers and citizenship of the Kingdom is established through adoption by the King, our identity and allegiance are changed forever. We are now the "God people" in which the Spirit resides. Jesus is calling citizens today to "leave behind other allegiances in favor of following after Him, to join a community [colony] of those who have left 'the world,' and to announce and practice the Kingdom of God – on earth as in heaven."[91] In Jesus we can now leave the empires of this world; they no longer have mastery over us.[92] Citizens must turn away from false allegiances and unhealthy dependencies or else they will never be able to live fully and effectively as agents of the Kingdom.

One other thing we must address before moving on is the temptation to be overly identified with the systems of this world. We all find some degree of satisfaction and camaraderie in our social class, political party, earthly nationality, church denomination, networks, or other groups that we gravitate toward. However, all of these must take a backseat to our ultimate allegiance. Yes, we have an earthly nationality. Yes, we align ourselves politically in light of our experience and beliefs. Yes, we get along better with certain types of people. But these ideologies or human systems in which we take part must not overshadow our identity as citizens. As we said in chapter one, the lens by which we now see the world and enter into these human arrangements is

91   Ekblad, *A New Christian Manifesto*, p. 93.
92   Romans 6.

the lens of Kingdom. The temptation is to focus on what is temporary and react to what is currently going on in our situation. How quickly we lose sight of the bigger picture. We allow our circumstances to dictate how we behave, instead of allowing our beliefs and identity to change the way we see. Nationalism or denominationalism can creep into a citizen's way of thinking, and before we know it, our initial response – our "gut" reaction – is to respond to situations according to our nationality or population segment. I can't tell you how many people I have met who blame things on their being British or American, etc. Of course, it is so much more than that, but they have simplified it into an easily identified label. But this is not where our ultimate allegiance lies. At the great throne of judgment, God is not going to ask us how well we did representing the Anglicans or the Americans. He is looking for something far beyond these human constructs.

This leaving of "the world" and transferring of allegiance to Jesus and His Kingdom is a process. It is the new reality of the believer the moment Jesus becomes King of their life, but it is also a reality that is realized over time. Theologians call it the process of sanctification: the business of becoming more like Jesus. We all are on a journey, and God's goal for the life of the citizen is that he or she would be molded into the image of Jesus.[93] This molding doesn't happen overnight. This shaping, this transferring of allegiance, is better known

93   Romans 8:29.

in the modern Christian world as discipleship.

Transferring allegiance to King Jesus is a proactive discipline, not a reactive one. Imagine a manual car parked on a steep hill. The moment the hand brake is pulled, that car is going to roll back down that hill. In neutral, there is no stopping gravity from taking its toll and the car from rolling down to crash at the bottom. The only thing that is going to make that car move forward is for someone to push the clutch, put the car into gear, and accelerate. In the same way, if the citizen is not proactively engaging with the King and His colony, and yielding to the Spirit in their life, they will soon be rolling downhill to be absorbed into the culture of "the world." To live in neutral is to roll down the hill; to do nothing is to roll down the hill. The only thing that wills the citizen forward is intentionality mixed with grace.

I love the way Paul explained it to the colony in Ephesus; he wrote this:

> It wasn't so long ago that you were mired in that old stagnant life of sin. You let the world, which doesn't know the first thing about living, tell you how to live. You filled your lungs with polluted unbelief, and then exhaled disobedience. We all did it, all of us doing what we felt like doing, when we felt like doing it, all of us in the same boat. It's a wonder God didn't lose his temper and do away with the whole lot of us. Instead,

immense in mercy and with an incredible love,
he embraced us. He took our sin-dead lives and
made us alive in Christ. He did all this on his
own, with no help from us! Then he picked us up
and set us down in highest heaven in company
with Jesus, our messiah…

That's plain enough, isn't it? You're no
longer wandering exiles. This kingdom of faith
is now your home country. You're no longer
strangers or outsiders [non-citizens]. You *belong*
here, with as much right to the name Christian
as anyone. God is building a home. He's using us
all – irrespective of how we got here – in what he
is building. He used the apostles and prophets
for the foundation. Now he's using you, fitting
you in brick by brick, stone by stone, with Christ
Jesus as the cornerstone that holds all the parts
together. We see it taking shape day after day – a
holy temple built by God, all of us built into it, a
temple in which God is quite at home.[94]

Paul says that we used to let "the world" tell us how to live,
and it didn't work. But by grace, King Jesus stepped in and
embraced us. He took us from death to life, clothed us in
royal righteousness, and is fitting us together in a new home,
a new Temple, in which He dwells – the citizens' assembly

94 Ephesians 2:1–6; 19–22 (*The Message*).

(the church). The apostle Peter explains it this way: "[Now] you are a chosen people, a royal priesthood, a holy nation, God's special possession, that you may declare the praises of him who called you out of darkness into his wonderful light."[95] Discipleship, becoming more like Jesus, living the intentional life, is what makes us further realize and live on the basis of this allegiance.

What does this look like in reality? It looks like intentionally spending time with other citizens. Real time. Real life. Authenticity is the key here. What good is getting together with a bunch of Christians every week if you never actually talk about what is really going on? How can that be helpful? I actually find that destructive rather than constructive. Authenticity involves choosing to place yourself at the feet of more mature citizens who have gone before you, and opening your life and your heart, your dreams and your desires to them to ask the hard questions and to examine your motives. It means letting people in and not shutting them out. It means that becoming like the King is a "win" for you, not arranging your life to satisfy your fleshly desires. And it entails risk. I have had a number of friends who want this type of intentional relationship but are unwilling to put themselves out there and initiate ir. It's the classic case of Eeyore from the Winnie-the-Pooh stories by A. A. Milne. They want it, but mope around feeling sorry

95   1 Peter 2:9 (NIV).

for themselves instead of taking the initiative and seeking it out. It's as if they think someone is going to find them in a crowded store, grab them by the hand, and say to them, "I like you. I want to start an intentional gospel-centered relationship with you. Meet me at Starbucks at 10 a.m. tomorrow... and bring your Bible." I'm not saying God can't do that, but it's probably not going to happen that way! It takes courage to put yourself out there and initiate. But after all, what's the worst thing that could happen? They can say no. Big deal. Trust me, it is worth the risk.

What happens when we do not intentionally place ourselves at the feet of the community and proactively seek out intentional relationships with others who are also trying to leave "the world" and live in the alternative Jesus Kingdom?

Our culture disciples us.

The culture of the Western world makes so much noise that if there is no intentionality we will be drowned out. Adopted royal citizens of the Kingdom who are left to the whims and fads of culture, after enough exposure, get stripped, beaten down, and infiltrated. We become disciples of the culture and not of the King. I recently attended a seminar on the relationship between discipleship and the digital age in which we live. The presenter's argument was: "What people choose to feed themselves on affects who they become." He argued that in the consumer culture of the West, for the first time in the history of the world, the amount of information we see and hear per day (noise) and the way in which we receive it (networks, friends, celebrities, social media) have turned us into media consumers who gobble it all up with little to no time for questioning the ethics and impact.[96] The number of people registered as Facebook users, and on Twitter, Instagram, YouTube, and other social media sites, is phenomenal. On the tube in East London recently, I read an article in the *Daily Mail* about a new study that had determined that, on average, people with smartphones check them more than sixty times per day.[97] We live in a new age. We are constantly bombarded with messages, stories, news, information, gossip, music, videos, texts, emails, and photos, and they are all coming through a device we hold in the palm of our hand that we are checking sixty times a day. What people choose to feed themselves on affects who they become. Distraction is one of the mightiest of tools of the Enemy, and in our consumerist digital culture, if we are not intentional, we fall prey.

According to a recent study that analyzed Twitter users and content, "0.05% of the user population attract almost 50% of all attention on the social networking site."[98] Who

96   Rich Wilson, "Discipleship in a Digital Age," (article), Spring Harvest 2013.
97   "It's Probably Better to Talk: How checking our Phones 60 Times a Day is Driving Away Friends," *Daily Mail,* December 1, 2012.
98   Reuters Blog: http://blogs.reuters.com/felix-salmon/2011/10/03/is-twitter-dominated-by-0-05-of-users/

do you think the majority of the top 0.05% of users that everyone is following are? Celebrities, you've got it. What this means is that the top echelon of Twitter users whom the others are following is accounting for almost 50% of the content on the site. Or in plainer language, the celebrities, the athletes, the pop stars are the people by whom the average person reading their tweets is being bombarded and informed. It's not the celebrities' fault that millions of people want to listen to them and find out what they are up to. But it is the citizens' problem if overexposure to this racket assists in weakening our allegiance. In this instance, that 0.05% can become the cultural disciplers of our day.

We live in a world that is upside down. The way it is now is not the way it was originally created to be. As humans living post-Eden, we are subject to the effects of the fracturing of the planet and the consequences of sin.[99] Much as in Rome, in the West today, power, fame, wealth, and status still have immense influence on society. The true King came to show humanity what earth looks like when God is in charge. In Jesus, this Kingdom way of life was exemplified on earth, and by living that way, He was subverting the religion of the day (Judaism) and the empire. Jesus is about the business of putting the world to rights, of putting it back together the way it is supposed to be – turning it right side up – and He is inviting us to do the same. Our allegiance to the true King

99   Genesis 3.

is a call to subvert the empires of the world. In Jesus, we are being trained to see, and life is a matter of seeing before it is a matter of doing.

6

A Citizen's Choices

"The way we understand human life depends on what conception we have of the human story. What is the real story of which my life story is a part?"[100]

Lesslie Newbigin

"I will place no value on anything I have or may possess except in relation to the Kingdom of Christ."

David Livingstone

Caesar Augustus ruled the Roman world from 31 BC to AD 14.[101] After his death, he was deified just like his adoptive father, Julius Caesar. Augustus' successor, Tiberius, took on

100 Lesslie Newbigin, *The Gospel in a Pluralist Society*, Grand Rapids: Eerdmans,1989, p. 15.
101 Tom Wright, *Simply Jesus*, p. 30.

the same title and pronounced himself *Augustus Tiberius Caesar, Divi Augusti Filius*, or "Augustus Tiberius Caesar, son of the Divine Augustus."[102] He too was a son of a god. Part of the Roman way of showing their domination to all of their subjects was erecting monuments and statues of the emperor throughout the empire, and issuing currency with the emperor's portrait on it. Tiberius' coinage had a portrait of him on one side, along with the inscription mentioned above, and on the reverse side was a picture of Tiberius dressed as a priest, with the title "Chief Priest" in Latin.[103] This was a subtle reminder to everyone in the empire of who was in charge, and of course further repulsed the Jews living under Roman occupation. This coin of Tiberius, with his inscription on it, is about to bring us into a discourse with widespread ramifications.

The other significant party that were in direct opposition to Jesus during His time on earth, about whom we have as yet said little, were the Jewish religious authorities. To oversimplify the story leading up to their conflict with Jesus, we must first understand the history of Israel. Israel was God's chosen nation; they had been given a name, a people, a land, and a promise, and for centuries they had been awaiting the long-promised messiah who would come for His people and punish evil and uphold righteousness (as

102 John F. Walvoord and Roy B. Zuck, *The Bible Knowledge Commentary*, Victor Books, 1983: Mark 12:16 passage.
103 Tom Wright, *Simply Jesus*, p. 30.

represented by them). This messiah would come and put everything right. He would deliver His people from years and years of slavery and oppression, and do away with their enemies who lived contrary to the ways of God. Much as in the story of Passover and the exodus from the hands of Egypt, the promised messiah would come to deliver them once and for all. He would defeat the wicked, restore the Temple, and dwell with His people once again. This long-awaited messiah King would definitely not come into town on a peasant's donkey.

One day in Jerusalem, a day or two after riding into town on a donkey, Jesus was approached by the Pharisees, who intended to trap Him with His own words. The Pharisees were a leading Jewish political and social group who believed in strict observance of the Old Testament law. Maintaining the law and thus remaining holy and pure were of the utmost importance to this group, and this of course became the fuel for serious accusations directed toward this rebel Jesus, who was a rabbi yet operated in an otherworldly manner. On this day, the Pharisees sent their delegates, along with some from other Jewish groups, to Jesus to ask Him a question: "Teacher, we know that you are truthful and do not court anyone's favor, because you show no partiality but teach the way of God in accordance with the truth. Is it right to pay taxes to Caesar or not? Should we pay or shouldn't we?"[104] Basically:

104 Matthew 22:16–17 (NET Bible™).

"Jesus, is paying tribute tax to Rome lawful?" They asked this hoping to entrap the would-be rebel messiah with His own answer. Now, to understand this question and Jesus' answer accurately, we have to get past our modern assumption that there was a separation between religion and politics, for there definitely was not. The Pharisees and the Herodians (the other Jewish sect present) knew that according to Jewish law it was not lawful to pay tribute to Rome. "They also would have known that not to pay the tribute would have been taken by the Romans as tantamount to rebellion."[105] And in Rome, rebellion equaled suicide. These guys had put Jesus in a tough spot, and in public; they knew full well what they were doing. Jesus saw this all going down and responded, "Hypocrites! Why are you testing me?"[106] He then asked them to show Him a common coin that was used every day. So they brought Jesus a denarius with Caesar Tiberius' portrait and inscription on it. Jesus looked at the coin, held it in His hand, and read the inscription: "Tiberius: son of god" and "Chief Priest" and then asked them, "Whose image is this, and whose inscription?"[107] They responded, "Caesar's." Then Jesus very authoritatively said to them, "Then give to Caesar the things that are Caesar's, and to God the things that are God's."[108] They all left stunned and amazed.

Jesus didn't say outright that paying tribute tax to Rome

105 Horsley, *Jesus and Empire* (Kindle Locations 1271).
106 Matthew 22:18 (NET Bible™).
107 Matthew 22:20 (NET Bible™).
108 Matthew 22:21 (NET Bible™).

was unlawful. He was much shrewder than that, although every Israelite listening to this conversation, including the Pharisees, would have interpreted it that way. If God is the true and exclusive master of the planet, then all things belong to Him… including everything that Caesar claimed for himself. Jesus was making a strong statement that Caesar, or any other world ruler, had no claim on Israel, since God was their ultimate master. Even if we are to take Jesus' words literally, then He was effectively saying the same thing from a broader perspective. "Pay Caesar what the law requires of you, but God owns all and allows rulers to rule in the first place;" "Pay Rome the due tax for living in the empire, but give God your ultimate allegiance." Either way, God demands exclusive loyalty.

This Scripture excerpt from Matthew 22 provokes a much-needed question at this point in our journey. How do we as citizens of God's Kingdom, people who pledge our allegiance to Him, live in a world in which we have other loyalties, responsibilities, and even allegiances? How are we to decide what is best or most honoring to God when given a choice between two different options? Many of us have spouses with whom we have entered into a covenant, families to which we are loyal, and employers to whom we are responsible, and all of us have earthly nations that we represent and cultures that we naturally align ourselves with. We are people with compounded loyalties.

I have a friend who was run over by a red double-decker London bus. Ryan and I met one day at a football pitch in northeast London (soccer for you non-English). Actually, to put it better, the Holy Spirit arranged our meeting. I was jogging through Redbridge, the London borough in which we live, and was cutting through the football fields to get to another road for my return home. I had my headphones in and was trying to keep up my pace when I noticed a guy in his late teens kicking a football around by himself in the middle of the field. I continued my jog, passed him, and then felt a very strong prompting by the Spirit to go and talk to this young man for some reason. I ignored the prompting and kept on jogging, but the feeling persisted. So I stopped to do business with God: "Are You serious? Right now? I'm trying to keep my heart rate up. You are omniscient; You should know this!" After a bit of a heart check, God won, and I jogged over to Ryan. In the most "unstalkerlike" way that I could manage, I walked up to him and asked if I could play football with him. He agreed and we struck up a basic conversation before he had to leave to go home. Before he went, he asked for my number so that next time he and his mates got together to play, they could give me a ring and have me come over to join them.

Sure enough, Ryan rang, and I went back a few times to meet him and his mates for a kick around. I probably saw him three more times, and over that period he called or texted me on average five times a week. I was beginning to regret being obedient to God. It was like being a university minister all over again, only this time I had to play each message multiple times to decipher the heavy East-End accent. This went on for a few weeks, and then it stopped… suddenly. No more calls. No more texts. Ryan went dark. I didn't hear from him for over a month.

When Ryan rang me after this prolonged period of no transmission, he sounded weak and out of it. I asked him what was going on and if he was OK. Ryan informed me that the last time I had seen him at the football pitch, I had gone one way to go back to my car, and he the other to walk home. He stepped out to cross the street, didn't see the double-decker bus coming, and it hit him head on. Ryan went flying, ended up on the opposite side of the street, and was immediately rushed to the emergency room and put into an induced coma to increase his chance of survival. Weeks passed with him lying in this induced coma, and when it looked as if he was miraculously going to make it back, they woke him up. He had a broken leg, hip, and collarbone, and some serious internal bleeding and bruising. But he had made it.

The next time I saw Ryan, we were back on the football pitch. Despite our two-month hiatus we were able to reconnect, and I asked him all my questions: "How did it happen?" "What do you remember?" As he gave me the details it became very clear to me that Ryan ought not to be alive. He should not have made it through this. I felt that I should tell him this. And as I did, tears welled up in his eyes, and he said something profound. "You know, Rob, it's as if I was spared for something … for a reason. It's like I am special and I am supposed to do something with my life before I die." My missionary training immediately kicked in and I could not believe that God had set it up this way. The ball was on the tee, and God had given me the Big Bertha.

I would love to tell you that Ryan fell to his knees, repented of his own sin and that of his generation, pulled out his wallet and gave everything he had to the poor, memorized the Gospel of Mark, and got a cross tattoo on his forearm all before leaving the pitch … but he didn't. He just listened.

Ryan will never fully know why a bus hit him one day as he walked home. I will never completely understand why I was led to speak with him in the first place. You will never know why you were born the year you were, into the specific family you were, and in that specific geographical location. You can spend your entire life wondering about it, but you will never fully know.

For many of the particulars of our lives, we will never know the "Why?" A much better question to direct our thoughts and energy toward is, "What now?" I think we have become really good at asking the wrong questions.

It's no different with our loyalties. "Why do I give forty hours of my week to this job I don't really feel fulfilled by and honestly don't care about, and as a result am too tired and worn out to give anything to my family and church?" "Why do I love my job, but am not at all excited about the opportunities to serve in my church community?" "Why am I most energized by studying and applying myself to academia, but when it comes to people I get exhausted?" "Why does it seem that the 'holy things' or 'God things' I should care about, such as evangelism or serving at church, are really the last things on my list of life-enhancing activities?" Our divided loyalties can bring us much confusion and guilt when not looked at correctly.

Both the ancient Greeks and the Romans tended to separate faith and beliefs from the rest of their life, and so do most people today. Known to academics as "dualism," this way of thinking "seals off personal beliefs and faith from the way we actually live and work in the world."[109] If we follow this train of thought, what we will end up believing is that direct forms of ministry such as teaching, evangelizing, discipling, and helping in the children's church are the only ways to serve God, while the outside or "secular" world is bad and polluting. We think that if we want to love Jesus, we need to get really good at and invest our time in the "sacred" things, while minimizing the number of "secular," worldly things that we take part in. To exaggerate the point, the world is bad, God is good, so God's people need to spend

109 Tim Keller, *Gospel in Life: Grace Changes Everything*, Zondervan, 2010, p. 159.

their time doing good things, as Jesus did, and not bad things, as non-citizens do. This thinking can carry over into the way we view our loyalties as well: "I am loyal to my job, but more loyal to Jesus... therefore, I should quit my job to minister within the church, where God's real work is being done." Or: "I am loyal to my country, but more loyal to Jesus, and we need to get back to operating on godly principles as a nation, so until we do, I am going to home-school my kids and remove myself from 'secular' society as far as I can."

We see this type of thinking creeping into the colony as well. The real spiritual or "sacred" work is done up front by the preacher and the "worship leader," while the lesser acts of service are carried out by the normal people. "Let the 'professional Christians' do the heavy spiritual lifting while you (the average believers) just make sure you give your money and invite people every once in a while to what we are doing here at the church. I'm sure you know that Jesus uses only well-spoken, theologically trained people to do significant things for the Kingdom"... This is, of course, a completely ridiculous way of thinking.

The gospel in no way supports a "sacred" and "secular" distinction. In fact, the gospel message is exactly the opposite. Jesus died, and the veil separating the "Holy of Holies" from the common area in the Temple was torn.[110] Because of Jesus, no longer did people enter the Temple to

110 Luke 23:45.

meet with God, but God now dwelled within them. The gospel is a proclamation that no longer is there a divide between "sacred" and "secular." Jesus infiltrates all of your life and desires to penetrate every sphere in which you are active. Therefore, Christianity is not simply a set of beliefs to adhere to in order to save your individual soul and escape the world at death or the rapture, but is actually a new way of seeing (and experiencing) everything in the world.

Are we artists, baristas, teachers, electricians, engineers, students, or factory workers who also just happen to be citizens of the Kingdom? Or are we, first of all, citizens of the Kingdom who happen to serve vocationally in these ways?

Our baseline for living has been changed to a Kingdom baseline. The gospel and the Father's Kingdom are now the foundations for the citizen, and all of our other loyalties are to be viewed through this lens. When this lens is used, we can clearly see that a job as a banker can be just as glorifying to God and just as Kingdom-focused as the life of a missionary out witnessing every day. For the citizen, it is about who you are and how you live, not about your title or job description.

The Kingdom life is evaluated according to a different set of criteria from the systems of "the world." Back when I was studying in seminary, I had a professor who allowed his students to contract for the grade they wished to obtain. At the beginning of the semester, he would hand out a chart that laid out how many papers and what type of mark would be necessary to achieve the desired grade. For instance, if you wanted an "A" then you would need to do four papers and pass with an average grade of ninety or more. For a "B" you would do only three papers with an eighty-five average, and so forth. What struck me most is not that I contracted to get "B's" in that class, but that at the beginning of the year he told us that for some of us to get an "A" in his class would be sinful. He said, "Some of you are married and have kids and other responsibilities, and if you contract for an 'A' in my class that would be sinning. Others of you, you single guys, if you contract for a 'B' or 'C,' that would be sinning. You know your priorities and where God has placed you in life right now, so contract accordingly." That really resonated with me. He was saying that if I neglected my new wife and my wider ministry for the sake of an "A" in his class, then my priorities were probably not right. In the Kingdom, the criteria by which we evaluate "success" are often countercultural.

I would love to include a checklist at the back of this book that would provide you with a sure way of living out your allegiance to King Jesus in the most honoring way possible. All you would need to do is follow this easy, step-by-step guide and tick the boxes along the way. Unfortunately, I can't. God didn't set it up that way. Life is not always black and white. Living as a citizen of the Kingdom often takes you into the "gray." And it is in the "gray" that we are forced to live by faith. As we have learned from the previous chapters, we can most definitely state, though, that when we worship Jesus and proclaim Him as Lord, we are strongly implying that no one else is in that position.[111] Our ultimate allegiance is to Jesus, and from that baseline our other loyalties flow and are influenced. I can't give you a checklist, but God has given you something much greater. He has given you Himself.

The Holy Spirit, the Counselor, the Sent One, takes up residence in the citizen. He is the down payment on your salvation and the promise that God is not ever going to leave or forsake you. Following the Spirit's leadings, yielding to His desires, evaluating your actions and decisions with the creator of the universe living in you is God's way of ensuring that you have the ability to live out your allegiance well. Jesus actually said that it is to *your advantage* that He does not physically walk alongside you, showing the way, but that He takes up residence within you.[112] This is huge: God, inside you, woven into all of your being, leading you into His truth. Yes, we are people with multiple loyalties and commitments in a world that pulls at us from all angles. Yes, it can be daunting and confusing at times. But we serve a King who sent Himself off to die for His people, and then, even greater, gave Himself to us so that we don't have to go through this life on our own.

Citizen, the Spirit is your compass, guiding you through your priorities, loyalties, and commitments. You

111 Tom Wright, *Simply Jesus*, p. 215.
112 John 16.

were given it as a symbol of your allegiance to the King. It is supernaturally calibrated always to point you to what is true and right. You have it, but it is of no use to you if you don't allow it access and a voice to speak. In the same way, learning to listen to it takes practice. It is an art. The more time you spend listening, the easier it will become. The true beauty comes when you find yourself in the middle of your daily activities or conversations and simultaneously listening to the Spirit and taking your cues from above. It is in this dance with God between citizen and Spirit that the real joy is found… where you begin to let go, and He begins to lead.

7

Part-time Citizens

"Jesus was not crucified for saying or doing what made sense to everyone."[113]

Hauerwas and Willimon

"A life changing love is inconvenient."[114]

Tim Keller

During my undergraduate studies I had a friend named Josh. Josh didn't go to the same university as me, but to our big rival about a hundred miles away. I could tell you quite a few stories about the mischief the two of us got into over the years, but there is one story that stands out among the rest. You see, Josh and I went to secondary school together and remained friends through the first few years of university, even though we were at hated rival schools.

113 Hauerwas and Willimon, *Resident Aliens*, p. 110.
114 Tim Keller, *Gospel in Life: Grace Changes Everything*, DVD sermon.

It all started one afternoon when Josh decided to ride his motorbike down the highway for the one-hundred-mile journey to Austin, Texas, where I was enrolled to study business at the University of Texas. I heard a knock at the door of my dorm room and when I went to answer, to my surprise, there he stood, helmet and gloves still on, fresh from the road, ready to hang out. Apparently he was going to stay for the weekend, which was no problem for me because I didn't have much planned for Saturday and Sunday. That Saturday night is when it all went down, and I now have a story to tell my kids when they are older about how to not be stupid for the sake of adventure.

We had just finished watching the university football match (American football), and on the way back to my dormitory, Josh nonchalantly said, "Have you ever been to the State Capitol?"

"Once when I was a kid," was my reply. For those of you not familiar with Texas, Austin is the state capital and the Capitol building is literally right next door to the university campus. Josh continued on with his persuasion: "I was with my mom one time and we found an unlocked door to the Capitol building... all you have to do is open it and you can get a free tour of everything. We should go!" Always up for a new adventure, I agreed, and off we went. The fact that it was 9 p.m., the building was surely closed, and you were supposed to sign up for a guided tour days in advance didn't really cross my mind at the time.

We walked down toward the Capitol and before we reached the building, about 200 meters from it, Josh led me down a staircase to a door that looked as if it led into an underground parking lot. We lifted the handle and the door flung wide open. Sure enough, it was unlocked! Josh's mom was right. At this point, I began to get pretty nervous, because I had thought he was pulling my leg the entire time. Now this secret personal walking tour of the Capitol building at night was getting very real. We walked through the doors to find an array of black SUVs and Mercedes Benz cars that I assume were used by members of the Texas Congress and the recently resigned Governor George Bush's entourage. (This was the same Governor Bush who was Governor of the State of Texas and then went on to become the 43rd President of the United States.) We walked through this parking lot past the rows of cars, and when we both agreed that we thought we were actually under the Governor's Mansion (it is next door to the Capitol), we walked a little further to a door leading into the Capitol building. It was unlocked too. (Now I don't mean to give away any national or state security secrets, but I sincerely hope that whoever was in charge of locking the doors to this place has found new employment.) Josh and I slowly pushed the door open and entered directly into the rotunda that has a portrait of every person who has served as President of the Republic of Texas or Governor of the State. I just could not believe this. We were both a little unsure whether we should proceed, both secretly nervous but acting like confident alpha males, and both sweating. Looking back, this was the moment we made our mistake. We should have turned back and had a great story to tell the boys back at the dorm.

But we didn't. We carried on. Our goal was to find the Governor's office, sit at his desk with our feet up, and take a picture for the new social media website – America Online. As we walked slowly through the rotunda we noticed security cameras that we made sure to dodge. We also passed quite a few night cleaners, who we found spoke only Spanish. So in our best Spanish we asked them for "Silencio, por favor," while motioning with our index fingers over our lips. We continued to catwalk gingerly up each flight of stairs, dodging cameras and cleaning people, until we made it to a set of doors that read "Governor of the State of Texas." Josh and I looked at each other, half freaked out and half eager to push the doors open, all the while having an unspoken conversation of nods and winks that said, "We made it."

In a movie, we would have taken off our backpacks and planted a bomb under the desk and then phoned the President of the United States on an untraceable line to inform him that we were holding the country to ransom and had "taken" the Capitol of Texas. In reality, we just wanted a silly picture.

We pushed open the doors to the office, and then turned around dead in our tracks, stunned by two state troopers yelling at us to "Freeze!" This is the moment I soiled myself. OK, I didn't *actually* soil myself, but I did see an image of myself in federal prison wearing a black and white onesie. Josh and I engaged in some rapid rhetoric, trying to explain that we had been taking a tour and that the back door was unlocked. The more we talked, the more the troopers let down their guard, and five minutes later we had been escorted out of the building and told never to try anything like this again. I think it was a wise move for Josh to say that his mom had been the one who had found the unlocked door in the first place. By the time we reached civilian territory outside of the closed Capitol building, we were chatting with the troopers about the football game that had ended a few hours earlier. They were actually quite amazed that we had made it in that far unseen. Once our heart rates had returned to normal, the conversation ended with a verbal warning from the troopers, and Josh and I strolled back to the dorm in awe of what had just transpired. True story.

Like a lot of storytellers, I like to work in the good ones whenever possible, as best befits the conversation. For a long time after this night, in fact for at least three more years until I graduated, I liked to tell this story to my college friends and in their minds loosely associate myself with the then President of the United States. (We snuck into the

Governor's office in my first year at uni, and the following year George W. Bush was elected President.) So, whenever the inauguration was on television, "Oh man, I haven't seen that guy's picture since I saw it in the Governor's office at the Capitol ...," that kind of thing. But even though I could *very* vaguely associate myself with him, I had never met him. I went to school close to his house, his daughter was in one of my classes, I had been to a baseball game where he had sat ten rows in front of me behind home plate, I had been in his old office, I even voted for him, but I didn't know him.

It is distressingly easy for churchgoers to do exactly the same thing.

Many of us attend church, celebrate Easter, get our children baptized, say a prayer before meals, have a favorite passage of Scripture, tick Christianity in the "religious beliefs" section of a questionnaire, and might even attend a small group, but we don't *know* King Jesus. There is a significant difference between association and relationship.

In the West, we are increasingly surrounded by a consumer culture. It is a "buy now, get what you want when you want it; have it your way, the customer is always right" culture. And this is killing the church. Unfortunately, churchgoers are often infiltrated by "the world" and are influenced to live in a manner just as consumerist as that of those on the outside. What really hurts the colony is that consumerism has made it socially acceptable to just add

Jesus to what you are already doing. Live your life how you wish, but go to church to honor the King on Sundays. Speak to people how you wish, but make sure to say "God bless" at the end of the conversation. Gossip about your friends and family and those in the colony, but phrase it in such a way that you can say you are sharing a "prayer request." Buy the latest Christian books and music, have them on your shelves and on your iPhone, but don't allow them to affect how you live. After all, it is your life. Only do what is comfortable.

Allegiance to King Jesus is a personal relationship, not a vague association. It is an all-or-nothing lifestyle, not a pick-and-choose salad bar.

I think those of us in the colony all too easily forget that we are not *entitled* to citizenship. We are not owed a relationship with God. We are not owed profound yet humorous sermons week in and week out, with amazing heart-melting worship music that was written by the worship pastor, who quit his "secular" band to lead us personally every week. The greatest children's and youth programs, adult small groups, and world-class teaching are not our due because we are citizens. Mall-like facilities for our worship center, complete with coffee bar, are not what we should expect. Conversations at lunch after our Sunday service should not be about whether or not we got something out of the sermon or what we really did not like about the service today.

Why?

Grace is why.

Citizenship is available to us only because of the cross of the King. The adoption we experience, via the blood of Jesus, that brings us into the Kingdom is nothing we have earned, nothing we are owed, and nothing we consume.[115] Truly understanding that we were DEAD, but that by grace Christ has made us ALIVE, should stir up in us a profound love for what Jesus is all about. Actually, technically speaking, our life is no longer even our own.[116] We were bought at a price. It cost someone a great deal for us to be alive and transformed; it cost someone their life – and that someone was the King.

Here is the scary part. In Jesus' teaching known as the "Sermon on the Mount," He tells His hearers that in life there are two gates, only two, and everyone will be passing through one or the other. He explains, "Enter through the narrow gate. For wide is the gate and broad is the road that leads to destruction, and many enter through it. But small is the gate and narrow the road that leads to life, and only a few find it."[117] The two words in that short passage that are the most important in the entire sermon are "many" and "few." Jesus says that many will enter through the wide gate that is comfortable, spacious, easy, and unevaluated, and eventually leads to destruction. But only a few find the narrow gate and

115 Ephesians 2:8–9.
116 1 Corinthians 6:19–20.
117 Matthew 7:13–14 (NIV).

the road that leads to life. This road is, in the words of Eugene Peterson, "vigorous and requires total attention."[118] Here Jesus cuts to the point and simplifies what He is after: total allegiance.

He goes on in the following verses to explain that, on the day of final judgment,

> … not everyone who says to me, "Lord, Lord,"
> will enter the kingdom of heaven, but only he
> who does the will of my Father who is in heaven.
> Many will say to me on that day, "Lord, Lord, did
> we not prophesy in your name and in your name
> drive out demons and perform many miracles?"
> Then I will tell them plainly, "I never knew you.
> Away from me, you evildoers!"[119]

Jesus is saying that the Kingdom of heaven and true citizenship are not for those who claim the name of "Christian," but for those whose lives reflect that He is Lord. He says that, on this day, people will list all the things they did for God, in the name of God: the "churchy" things they were a part of, the things that made them talk, look, and act like followers, but the King will turn to them and say, "I never knew you." He will say to them, "I don't know who you are. You aren't one of Mine." These people will then go

118 Matthew 7:14 (*The Message*).
119 Matthew 7:21–23 (NIV).

over to stand in the queue at the entrance of hell.

My fear is that there are people reading this who identify themselves as a member of the colony, attend some sort of Christian gathering, and do many nice things for people, but in the end, when all is stripped away and things are made perfectly clear, are only associated with God. They might be "religious," but they do not know Him.

This is what religion does. It gives people a way of thinking and behaving so that they can be reassured that what they are doing is what God wants. If I think, act, dress, and do as everyone else in the church does, then I must be doing it right. The checklist proves that I am OK. Religion gives us a list of things we should do, and things we should not. Religion is based on how we perform, not on the truth that we are already accepted. It makes us proud of what we do, not of what Jesus has done. It preys on fear and insecurity, and is not founded on grace and joy.[120]

The vast majority of people I meet in London have no association with church. You have to go back two generations (to people's grandparents) to find a generation who were familiar with church and attended as part of their weekly rhythm. That's why the missiologists regard London as a post-Christian city. Most of the people I meet, if forced to think and then speak about Jesus, commonly view Him through the lens of religion and not of relationship. I

120 For more information on religion vs. gospel, check out Tim Keller's "Gospel in Life" material.

don't blame them. A brief history lesson on the church in England and the power, politics, and compromise between the church and the nation will ensure this result. This isn't a slur on the UK, but rather a commentary on what happens in any country when broken individuals lead a human organization that gets mixed up with politics. For too long, Jesus has been associated with "religion." In an effort to be politically correct and reach more people with the gospel, the gospel itself has actually become compromised, and now your average person on the street cannot distinguish the difference between the two.

For example, when I sit down with a new friend to discuss anything to do with spirituality and Jesus, I must first spend multiple meetings with them deconstructing "Christianity" as they know it. We talk through what Christianity is not, and debunk all those myths before we can reconstruct an accurate view of Jesus from the Gospels. We break down before we build up. We must confront why the church to them is a judgmental, irrelevant crutch for people who can't get their lives together on their own. We have to talk about why their child cannot get into the better church school in their parish (with more opportunities for its pupils) because they do not attend the church associated with it. We must deal with their uncle who was a minister who sexually abused them when they were a child. Not fun, but necessary. Religion and sin taint and confuse the message and person of Jesus.

The French enlightenment philosopher Voltaire once wrote, "Si Dieu nous a fait à son image, nous le lui avons bien rendu" (If God has made us in His image, we have returned the favor). This is an observation not only on how we view God in our own minds, but on how we collectively as humans have represented Him on earth. But the story of God revealed in Scripture is a grand narrative showing us that Jesus did not endure humiliation and death so that we could live life with Him on our own terms. Quite the contrary: following Jesus, living as a true citizen, is a radical new way of life that resists the wide-gate trap of fitting Jesus in only when it seems to work to our advantage.

One of the most damaging things we have done in Christendom (the "empire" of Christianity where the majority are assumed to be Christian) is to reduce following Jesus to a series of programs or events: To get more out of your relationship with Jesus, do _____. Come to our next event and hear about _____. Make sure to not miss our upcoming _____.

Coming from a church background, and being an ordained pastor, I do get why we have programs and events. God can definitely work through them, and He does. I am not anti-program or anti-event, but what I think has become our default position in the organized colony (the established church) is that following Jesus gets reduced to a step-by-step system that you need to go to church to engage in (or consume) in order to live the Christian life better. We have effectively taught people, probably inadvertently, that the real Jesus work happens on Sundays in the main service or at the big events. We spend most of our money and time working toward these "large-impact" events, to the detriment of life-on-life ministry taking place from Monday to Saturday. When Sunday slips into becoming "the show," and the rest of the week is just planning and work leading up to "the show," we have lost our focus. When our evangelism is reduced to inviting people to our weekend services, we have a problem. No wonder church people are behaving like consumers; we (church leaders) are treating them that way.

We are in desperate need of a re-examination, a rethinking, and a recommitting to our founder, King Jesus. When we break down all that Jesus taught, all that He desired for His called-out colony to become, and take a hard look at His life and plan for intentional ministry, it all comes down to the foundations of discipleship and commitment. Not flash and pomp, not a show, not a big-budget event or a well-executed program… it comes down to living a life of intentionality.

And non-intentional people = part-time followers.

Jesus said, "I am the way,"[121] and His concern was not with programs or events to reach the crowds, but "with

121 John 14:6.

men whom the multitudes would follow." People "were to be His method of winning the world to God."[122] Jesus spent His time with a few men and women, calling them to follow Him, intentionally spending time with them, and then releasing them to turn the world upside down. These disciples became citizens and observers of the Kingdom way of life as they walked and lived with Jesus. He modeled for them what heaven on earth was to look like, and then He took them aside to explain it to them. Jesus intentionally invested in people and with them; He gave Himself away. He told them that they were to have complete abandonment and commitment to Him if they truly wished to be His followers. And then, watch this: He expected them to reproduce.

Jesus' entire ministry on earth, His grand evangelistic strategy, was left in the fragile hands of broken normal people. Broken normal people committed to Him. These people would be given the indwelling Spirit, and Jesus' strategy to reach a lost world would be dependent on their faithfulness. He had no other plan.

Wow. If I had been one of those first disciples, I would have thought Jesus was absolutely insane. Number one: we are completely going against Caesar and the empire, and basically giving them the finger. Number two: He really thinks that we are up for this. Number three: His determining factors of "success" are rooted in faithfulness, commitment,

122 Robert E. Coleman, *The Master Plan of Evangelism*, Revell, 1994, p. 27.

intentionality, and love. Not glamorous. Not sexy. But true and right.

Back to us… nothing has changed. Living out our citizenship of the Kingdom in today's world is going to look much more like what was just described than merely showing up for a church service at the weekend. It's going to look like being faithful to God and the colony even when things aren't going our way. It means not jumping ship and leaving the community or trying to find another church to consume from when things don't go the way we think they should in our current church.[123] It means living intentionally. It means proactively seeking out other people to invest in us and for us to invest in. It means living a life of worship and justice. It is a life of sacrifice, of self-denial, of choosing to love, and putting our personal desires on the altar as a sacrifice to the King.

There was no such thing as a part-time citizen of the Roman empire, and according to Jesus, the same is true in the Kingdom.

---

123 I do not mean, however, to suggest that it's never right to change church. If the teaching becomes unbiblical, you feel you no longer have anything to contribute, or you feel called to serve elsewhere, it may well be the right thing to do.

8

Citizens as Ambassadors

"The primary action of the church in the world is the action of its members in their daily work."[124]
Lesslie Newbigin

"It's not so much that the church has a mission, it's that the mission of God has a church."[125]
Alan Hirsch

"Our Father in heaven, hallowed be your name. Your kingdom come, your will be done, on earth as it is in heaven."[126]
Jesus

124 Lesslie Newbigin, "Evangelism in the Context of Secularization," chapter in *The Study of Evangelism*, various authors, Eerdmans, 2008, p. 51.
125 Alan Hirsch, "What is a Missional Church?," Lecture, Verge Network. http://www.youtube.com/watch?v=Zv-Hpx-5Ye4 April 2, 2012
126 Matthew 6:9–10 (ESV).

There is a church across the street from my house that was built in 1909. A congregation began worshiping there in 1910, and in the Second World War it was completely destroyed when it was hit by bombs aimed at the nearby Canary Wharf docks and the ammunition factories there. Many of the bombs were off target and forty of them landed in my neighborhood, hitting the church and my house. Consequently, both of them were rebuilt much later, and now the neighbors on our street affectionately refer to our home as the "new" house on the street. It was rebuilt in the 1950s and looks nothing like the rest of the homes on the estate. (I never thought I would live in a "new" house that is more than sixty years old.)

When we moved in, we made friends with the minister of the Baptist church across the street, who was about to retire. We held our older son, Liam's, third birthday party in his church hall, and in return for our not having to pay to hire the hall, the pastor agreed that I would fill in for him and preach the next time he was away. Sounded great to me... I am always up for bartering rather than parting with hard cash.

Anyway, I got a call from the pastor one day and was asked to preach for him while he was away on holiday. I made plans to be there with the aging congregation that Sunday, and asked our worship leader to join me to lead the sung worship... kind of a tag-team duo approach.

Hai, our worship leader, had just finished touring the U.S. with some big Christian bands and was serving with us in London for a year as he transitioned out of the Christian music industry in America. Hai was given a hymnal to browse through to find some songs that the congregation might know. I left it with him, and together we showed up to lead that Sunday morning.

It turned out to be a very, shall I say, interesting morning. Beautiful on the one hand, but sad and depressing on the other. I came prepared to stand up and deliver the message I felt God had for us that morning. I was not expecting a large gathering, but when there were only five people (including the lady running the sound), I suggested pulling the chairs together for more of a facilitator-led Bible study. Preaching to fewer than twenty people is just awkward. Hai came with his guitar and PowerPoint slides, but after ten fruitless minutes of trying to get their old computer to play them, we ditched the slides and Hai decided just to play some old hymns on the guitar. In hindsight, I am pretty sure this was the first guitar that had ever made its way into that church. (Good thing we didn't bring a drummer, because everyone knows that drums are of the Devil…) We were definitely out of our comfort zone. We were the youngest people there by at least thirty years. Nevertheless, we went through the service as planned, and were lovingly embraced by this small remnant of faithful saints. We ended with tea and biscuits, heard some of the congregation's stories, and learned quite a few old English words that I now use to impress my friends.

Now, on the one hand, we met some beautiful and faithful committed members of the church that morning. A few of the elderly gentlemen told me story after story about what this church used to be like fifty years ago. They told me about their children being baptized in this church, how they used to have a Christmas celebration that the whole community would turn out for, and what this church needed to move forward. It was such a testimony to see people in their seventies who had been committed to the same church for their entire life. They had stayed with it over the decades, they prayed lovingly for it in our prayer time, and it was obvious that this church was central to their lives.

As Hai and I were making our way out, the sweet elderly woman in charge of the teapot cornered us. She was whipping out the teas, and if you didn't have more than one, I could sense that this would be a serious source of consternation for her. She thanked us for being there that morning, and then called to the others around her to tell us one last thing before we departed. "Rob, Hai… you know, the thing this church needs is an evangelist. If we could pool our money to hire an evangelist, he could knock on doors, hand out pamphlets, and reach those young families and others in the neighborhood. That's all we need… An evangelist like this would turn this church around. Will you be praying for this with us?" We drank our last sip of tea, thanked them, and walked across the street to my house.

Five seconds later, we opened the door to my home, where Hai and I were joined by Medea to evaluate the morning over lunch. "Did I hear this correctly?" I exclaimed. "Did they just say that in order to reach this community, they need to hire an evangelist to do the work for them?" Hai agreed that this was the gist of what we had heard them say. This was their plan to rejuvenate the congregation and be Jesus to this community. This was the other side of the story that morning.

This congregation is barely hanging on and their services are actually held in the church hall because the church building itself was condemned some twenty years ago. The once-thriving church's building now lies in ruins. At some point in the history of these believers' gathering together, mission work ceased to exist, and the current group now wants to "outsource" the outreach. Any hope of living out the gospel, putting faith into action, and leading others into the Kingdom rests now on the shoulders of an individual who probably will never be employed.

This church only embodies and epitomizes a frighteningly common mindset that many of us have in the church in the West. It is very easy for us to get so caught up in what is going on inside the colony that, before we know it, we have lost all real links with those outside. We outsource our mission because we are too busy working on ourselves. So many demands are imposed by the programs and Bible studies in which we take part that we have no time left to live intentionally outside of the camp. We have jobs, families, relationships, bills, busy calendars, and responsibilities: how can we make time for one more thing to do? How quickly our citizenship gets compartmentalized.

It can be argued that discipleship, viewed wrongly, can allow us to look only inward, but, viewed rightly, propels us outward. And it is in this propelling us out that we come to see and begin to live like Jesus, the first missionary. There is an old Latin phrase, *Missio Dei*, that scholars like to use. *Missio* comes from the verb "to send," and *Dei* means "of God." Therefore, *Missio Dei* is the sent-ness or mission of God. What this phrase means is that God is a missionary God. He sent Jesus into the world to live as a peasant King to deliver and reconcile the world to Himself. The Spirit too was sent from heaven to indwell citizens. God is a sending God.

Therefore, an unsent citizen is an oxymoron. There is no such thing. In John 20:21, Jesus is speaking to His followers and tells them, "Just as the Father has sent me, I also send you."[127] You are sent. I am sent. We are sent. Being sent out as King Jesus' ambassadors is non-negotiable: it's not just for the vocational missionaries or the super-holy; it is for everyone whom Jesus has claimed.

127 John 20:21 (NET Bible™).

It is now a part of your identity.

I've never met an ambassador of a country, but from what I understand, they not only represent their home country within the foreign one, but they also act on behalf of the one that has sent them. The ambassador is the resident who lives, represents, often speaks for, and conducts business as an agent of the sending authority. Effectively, they are an extension of the ruler or nation that they represent. When the apostle Paul was writing in 2 Corinthians chapter 5 he used this analogy to explain the sent-ness of the citizen of the Kingdom. He writes:

> Therefore, if anyone is in Christ, he is a new creation. The old has passed away; behold, the new has come. All this is from God, who through Christ reconciled us to himself and gave us the ministry of reconciliation; that is, in Christ God was reconciling the world to himself, not counting their trespasses against them, and entrusting to us the message of reconciliation. Therefore, we are ambassadors for Christ, God making his appeal through us. We implore you on behalf of Christ, be reconciled to God. For our sake he made him to be sin who knew no sin, so that in him we might become the righteousness of God.[128]

128 2 Corinthians 5:17–21 (ESV).

Paul's argument is fairly simple. You were dead. You have been reconciled to God. You have been transformed. Now you are being sent out to transform the world around you as an ambassador of the One who worked the transformation in you. You, citizen, are an ambassador of the King.

In the book of Acts an exchange between two very unlikely people is recorded, which forever altered salvation history on planet earth. Cornelius and Peter, one an upright moral Gentile and the other a Jew and apostle of Jesus, were destined by God to meet at a time when the mixing of their two peoples simply did not happen. Jews and Gentiles, broadly speaking, were enemies. To a Jew, Gentiles were an unclean, impure, unholy race. To a Gentile, the Jews were fanatical religious outsiders who lived in a pipe dream of elitism. Cornelius, however, although he was a Gentile, was known as a "God-fearer."[129] He was a righteous and moral person to whom God came in a vision, telling him to send for this man named Peter who lived in Joppa (about thirty miles away). Meanwhile, Peter is up on his rooftop in Joppa, we presume fasting and praying, when God also speaks to him in a vision. Peter falls into a trance and sees the heavens open up, and down comes a sheet with all kinds of unclean animals on it. And then the voice says, "Rise, Peter; kill and eat."[130] Peter thinks, "Surely not, these animals are unclean and this goes against the Jewish law." The voice continues,

129 Acts 10:2.
130 Acts 10:13 (ESV).

"Rise, Peter; kill and eat…" and this happens three times, and then the voice says, "What God has made clean, do not call common."[131]

While Peter is trying to figure out what on earth this means, the men whom Cornelius has sent to fetch him arrive. These men explain what has happened to Cornelius, and now the story gets interesting. Peter invites them in to be his guests. This is not normal. The next day, they all get up and make the journey to Caesarea and are welcomed into Cornelius' home. Again, this is unusual. Cornelius has invited his entire household over – family, relatives, workers, and close friends – in anticipation of Peter's arrival. After some welcoming exchanges, Peter jumps straight into what God has been revealing to him: "You yourselves know how unlawful it is for a Jew to associate with or to visit anyone of another nation, but God has shown me that I should not call any person common or unclean."[132] He continues explaining what has transpired over the last couple of days and then tells them that he now sees that God shows no favoritism. He goes on to tell them the gospel story, Jesus' life, death, and resurrection, and how they too may find forgiveness for sins and new life. Before Peter can even finish his message, the Holy Spirit falls on these Gentiles who now believe, and they are brought into the family of God.

The reason this was such a big deal is that, up to this

131 Acts 10:15 (ESV).
132 Acts 10:28 (ESV).

point, salvation in Jesus had been known only among the believing Jews of the day. This God-directed exchange revealed "the keys of the Kingdom" to the Gentiles, to give them citizenship and bring them into the colony. The door of faith was now open to all, and it was Peter whom God used as His ambassador to deliver the message.

I was preaching on this passage at the church my friend Paul leads one day when a guy named Adam was sitting in the congregation. Adam was not a regular at this church, as he had recently moved back into the area after a stint up in the north of England where he had been employed as a teacher. At some point during the message the Spirit began to stir Adam's heart, so he decided to make a deal with God – as we humans tend to do: "God, if You are trying to speak to me, I need You to give me a sign." Minutes later, Adam received a text message from the friend who had led him to the Lord, even though they had not seen one another in some years. The text read something like this: "Hey mate, I don't know what you are up to these days, but the Lord put it on my heart to pray for you just now… so just know that I am." Adam read this text and then began freaking out. I'm sure he did not hear anything else I said, and as soon as the service was over, this very excited Englishman came up to me bursting to tell me what had just transpired. I was thrown somewhat off balance, because my experience with the British in church up to this point had been that they were much more subdued and not very excitable. Adam was breaking the mold for me.

"Rob, Rob, I heard you talk… I got this text… Peter…. Cornelius… teacher… moved… God… friends… when do we start?!" That is pretty much all that I understood from this verbal outpouring of emotion. And although half of me was very skeptical, the other half was convinced that God was doing something in Adam.

Adam joined us the next Sunday evening in the missional community that we had just started. One thing you must know about Adam is that he is a connector. I'm sure you know the type. Adam knows everyone. He is constantly busy, a social butterfly, who talks first and thinks later, but his personality is so much fun that no one ever gets upset by what he says… that's just Adam. He had been with us for about a year when the guys in our community decided that we should go through a men's discipleship study of Robert Coleman's classic book, *The Master Plan of Evangelism*, which examines Jesus' model of discipleship and evangelism while on earth. We completed the study, and somewhere along the way it clicked for Adam. When we finished the last session, Adam was insistent that we start this course called Alpha with our friends who would never set foot in a traditional church. Alpha is basically a ten-week introduction to Christianity, based around a meal and conversation with a group of friends. After a little bit of planning, I invited everyone

I knew to come to our launch session, at which we would throw a party and then give a five-minute overview of what we would be doing over the following weeks, so that people could decide whether they wanted to come back. Medea invited all her friends; Robert (the Jerusalem rooftop guy) did the same, and so did everyone else in our community... including Adam.

The week leading up to our launch party, Adam was a nervous wreck. Understandably so: he was about to make a stand in front of all of his closest friends and reveal to them the most important person in his life: Jesus. Would they still want to be his friends after this? How would they react? Would they judge him? These are some of the questions that floated around in his mind all week. The night of the party came, and only one person showed up out of all the combined invites of Medea, Robert, and I. But then, to our amazement, twenty-six others who did not follow Jesus all came out to the launch. It was standing room only in the Peabody home that night, and as I made the rounds meeting people for the first time, it became very obvious that everyone there knew Adam. Many of them didn't know each other, but they all had Adam in common. That night, Adam was our Cornelius.

That evening there were thirty-plus people in our house discussing the things of God, many of them for the first time. As Medea and I cleaned up after they had all gone, we talked about what had just happened. It was very clear. The Spirit had grabbed hold of one guy, persuaded him to take a risk, motivated him to take advantage of all of his relationships, and as Adam put his faith into action that week, God had used him as an agent of the Kingdom.

It had been over a year since Adam and I had first met that Sunday I was preaching. A year God had used to shape and mold Adam's heart. A year of gently showing Adam that his story was to fit within the much larger story of God. A year in which he began to realize his new identity and allegiance to Jesus as a citizen of God's Kingdom. A year of learning what it meant to live as an ambassador and to make the most of what God had given for His Kingdom purposes. A year of finding joy in what it means to live the gospel.

When we hear stories like this one and the story of Peter and Cornelius, one of the things we tend to focus on is the proclamation of the citizen's message as the be-all and end-all. As ambassadors of the gospel, we are meant to herald Jesus' good news. This is undoubtedly true! It was the apostle Paul who said, "If you confess with your mouth that Jesus is Lord and believe in your heart that God raised him from the dead, you will be saved."[133] And a little further on in Romans 10 he explains that people cannot believe if they have not heard, and people cannot hear unless those who know Jesus' message speak and are sent out.[134] What a beautiful truth.

133 Romans 10:9 (ESV).
134 Romans 10:14–15.

However, from my observation of the circles in which I have moved in two different countries in the West, it seems that personal evangelism often gets elevated above personal justice. What I mean is that quite a bit of attention has been paid in the past few decades to personal salvation and the believer's duty to evangelize their lost friends, but the idea of the believer's getting involved in bringing about social justice has been narrowed down to only those who are interested in ministry among (for example) the homeless or orphans. We fail to acknowledge that ambassadors don't just proclaim; they also act. The gospel is not just about escaping hell and going to live in heaven forever when you die, but it is also (and just as importantly) about what you do while you are on this earth. One cannot be divorced from the other. The gospel is not only something you speak; it is also something you live. I don't mean to insult you with this clarification. I know you know this in theory, but too often we, both individually and corporately, don't live this way. Could it be that we don't fully understand biblical justice, or is this concept harder to swallow because of the uncomfortable changes it would require from us?

There is an old Hebrew word, *shalom*, which translates into English as "peace, wholeness, completeness," or "the way things ought to be." Our world was created with *shalom*. In the Garden in Genesis, everything fit together. It was complete and was exactly how God wanted it to be. Man and woman and all of creation were in harmony with one another and with God. Everything was right. But when sin entered the world this *shalom* was fractured. Brokenness and injustice, hurt and pain, wrongdoing and selfishness entered as the new reality of this world. Consequently, nothing is the way it should be: relationships, creation, our hearts, social systems, even the weather. They all exist naturally in a state of broken *shalom*.

Scripture tells us that because of the true King's death and resurrection, the world is now being put back to rights. There is a new creation bursting forth, made possible by the death and resurrection of God. The curse of broken *shalom* has been overthrown, and in Jesus, God's Kingdom has been launched on earth as in heaven. While on earth, Jesus was renewing, restoring, and redeeming all things – showing the world what it looked like when God was in charge. It's as if the world were under new management. He then invited His followers to take part in this work by sending them out to live as His ambassadors to make His Kingdom a reality.[135]

Therefore, Jesus was and is about restoring *shalom* in the world; He is setting it all back to rights. As we are now citizens of the Kingdom of heaven, Jesus invites us to do the same. United with Jesus, empowered by His Spirit, we have been transformed and now are sent out to live as restorers of social *shalom*.

135 Tom Wright, *Simply Jesus*, p. 193.

In Matthew 10 and Luke 10, Jesus gives instructions to his disciples before sending them out to be restorers of *shalom* for the nations. He tells them that they are to be carriers of peace as ambassadors of the Kingdom. Jesus instructed that when they approached a house they were first to declare their peace on it. If a person received their peace, they would be welcomed in and could share and minister to them. If they did not receive it, the disciples would move on to the next house, town, or city. In these sending narratives, Jesus is actively showing his followers that as ambassadors of the Kingdom, they carry with them this *shalom*. Not only are they looking for persons of peace to share with and through (like Cornelius), but the disciples themselves are now persons of peace. They are the peace bringers, the ones by which Jesus is sharing and demonstrating His Father's Kingdom.

As ambassadors of Jesus in the world today, who are also called to live as restoring agents of social *shalom*, we must begin by identifying what is broken. Sin and selfishness have corrupted this world, and every person, relationship, social structure, and sphere of activity has been marred. Power, greed, and self-interest have plundered these social structures, leaving weakness, inequality, and injustice behind them. We live in a world that is unfair. And engaging in doing justice means plunging ourselves into these weaker areas of society to begin righting the wrongs brought about by sin. Justice is love in action. It is disadvantaging yourself for the benefit of others.[136] It means identifying the injustices you come into contact with as situations where *shalom* has been broken, and doing something about it as Jesus' royal ambassador.

Another way of looking at doing justice is being a person who maximizes all that you have for the Kingdom. By grace, God has given you talents, skills, experience, your personality, and supernatural gifting. To some of you, he has given health and wealth, education, strong friends and families, and expertise in certain areas. To add action to your faith and to do justice is to identify where things are not right, not as they should be, and to take all that you have and use it to help rectify the wrongs that sin has caused. It means choosing not to use all the above-mentioned avenues of grace in your life for yourself and the people you love, but instead, choosing to disadvantage yourself to serve others (including those not like you). And by doing this, not only are you glorifying God in these situations, but you are literally acting on behalf of Jesus. Doing justice starts with seeing your life and the world around you through that different Kingdom lens.

The prophet Isaiah was told by God to get Israel's attention and confront them with this very issue. God's people had been praying, fasting, and seeking after Him in an

136 For more on this, read Tim Keller, *Generous Justice*, Zondervan, 2010.

effort to be near their Lord, but even after all of that, He still seemed distant. They couldn't figure out what the deal was. When they prayed, He didn't answer. When they fasted, He didn't seem to notice. They were doing all the "right" things, but God seemed ever further away. God then decided it was time to speak. He sent Isaiah to "Shout loudly!" and "Yell as loud as a trumpet!" to get their attention.[137] He meant what Isaiah was about to say to be heard as clearly as possible:

> The bottom line on your "fast days" is profit.
> You drive your employees much too hard.
> You fast, but at the same time you bicker and fight.
> You fast, but you swing a mean fist.
> The kind of fasting you do
> won't get your prayers off the ground.
> Do you think this is the kind of fast day I'm after:
> a day to show off humility?
> To put on a pious long face
> and parade around solemnly in black?
> Do you call *that* fasting,
> a fast day that I, God, would like?[138]

Here we see that Israel was engaged in all of the "right" activities, but their hearts and actions remained far from

137 Isaiah 58:1 (NET Bible™).
138 Isaiah 58:3–5 (*The Message*).

what God wanted. They had missed the point. God was not interested in their rituals and feasts; what He was really after was something very different. Isaiah goes on:

> This is the kind of fast day I'm after:
> to break the chains of injustice,
> get rid of exploitation in the workplace,
> free the oppressed,
> cancel debts.
> What I'm interested in seeing you do is:
> sharing your food with the hungry,
> inviting the homeless poor into your homes,
> putting clothes on the shivering ill-clad,
> being available to your own families.
> Do this and the lights will turn on,
> and your lives will turn around at once.
> Your righteousness will pave your way.
> The God of glory will secure your passage.
> Then when you pray, God will answer.
> You'll call out for help and I'll say, "Here I am."[139]

God wanted His people to disadvantage themselves for the enefit of others. He wanted them to employ all that they had to help right the wrongs that sin had created in society. He wanted His people to put the love they received from Him into action; to be conduits of that love. God wanted them

139 Isaiah 58:6–9 (*The Message*).

to do justice. If you look closely at the last sentence in this snippet from Isaiah chapter 58, you see that if God's people would begin taking it upon themselves to meet the needs of those around them, then God would be near. Later on in this passage it says that when God's people started actively helping the hungry and stepping in to help the oppressed, their light would "burst forth like the dawn."[140] Isaiah goes on to say that they would then find joy in their relationship with God and He would restore them.

What this passage reveals is that "… a lack of justice is a sign that the worshippers' hearts are not right with God."[141] In Isaiah 29, God says that these people who deprive the innocent of justice are people who "come near to me with their mouth and honor me with their lips, but their hearts are far from me."[142] In instance after instance in Scripture, God continually identifies Himself with the poor and the outcasts, and calls for His people to put their faith into action to do something about it. Alarmingly, He even states in Matthew 25 that our heart attitude toward the poor reveals our heart attitude toward Jesus.[143]

I wrote this chapter of the book while I was back in Texas for a week of meetings, and I was on a two-hour drive by myself to the airport when I decided to turn on the radio. I scanned through the different stations and finally settled

140 Isaiah 58:10 (my translation).
141 Keller, *Generous Justice*, p. 50.
142 Isaiah 29:13 (NIV).
143 Keller, *Generous Justice*, p. 53.

on the local Christian one to hear what type of music they were playing these days. As many of you know, in London Christian radio is much harder to come by, so this was a rare glimpse back into the evangelical subculture. As I was driving down the interstate a song came on by a well-known contemporary Christian artist whose lyrics were a proclamation of the fact that God is in you, and He is the same God who gives sight to the blind, clothes the naked, and frees the oppressed. It was catchy and had a good chorus, and I'm sure is a song that will lead people into worship as they listen to and contemplate the words. About thirty minutes later, still on the interstate, I started humming the tune to myself, which caused me to think more deeply about what was being said in this song. It dawned on me that it was all about God being the One who releases the captives and clothes the naked, but it never said how He does it. It was praising the God who can do these things, but then it just left it there. I found myself disheartened because this song epitomized what we often do in the colony. We ascribe glory to God for what He has done and can do, but then leave it at that until the next time we hear the song or go to church. It's like when we view a painting. We gaze at the beauty of the finished work and stand in awe of what was accomplished, but we rarely think about the hard work and hours upon hours of intentionality that went into making it so beautiful. God desires portraits of justice, and will see them accomplished, but He will be painting with people.

Sure, God could sit up in heaven and zap some naked person to clothe them instantaneously or zap an empty pantry so that it is miraculously filled with food, but He doesn't typically act that way. It's not His standard mode of operation. Instead, in His infinite wisdom, He has chosen to do these things... get ready... through PEOPLE. Now we all know this, but we act as if we don't. It's easier to sing about a God who is capable of doing justice than it is for His followers to participate and actually see it implemented. One of the most counterintuitive realities in the dance of life between the King and His citizens is that He is at work through *our* work.

As stated earlier, we live between the first advent and the next, and when King Jesus returns, He will pour out absolute and never-ending *shalom* on every inch of creation. In the meantime, we citizens are the Kingdom bringers. We are "Plan A" and there is no backup "Plan B" for Jesus' Kingdom expansion project on earth.

I want to propose to you that the proclamation of the gospel is tied up in this idea of justice. If justice is love in action, specifically righting the wrongs of the consequences of sin in our society (and there is no greater consequence of sin than spiritual separation from God), then our evangelism is a form of doing justice. Our evangelism opens the way for the hearer to receive the One who can restore, redeem, and bring completeness. It shows how they may be made right with God. It is an effort to give the answer that will right the wrongs of the sin *in* them. God desires, and the Kingdom needs, both proclamation and action. Personal evangelism and personal justice both flow from the heart of the yielded citizen.

So here we are. Because of the abundant, overflowing grace of God, He stepped into the mess we had made in which spiritual, emotional, relational, and societal *shalom* had been ruptured, and in Jesus broke the cycle once and for all. God died the death we should have died, and lived the life we should have lived. The cross changed history. Citizenship in Jesus and His Father's Kingdom was bestowed by faith, and the privilege was granted of representing Him to a fractured world. We live in the in-between, He will come for His people, but in the meantime, we are the Jesus people. We are the ambassadors. Proclaiming and acting in love, we speak and live out tangibly what it means to be a Kingdom people.

The powers of hell have been vanquished by our victorious King. The Enemy has been defeated and we eagerly await the final consummation of a new heaven and new earth, but in this in-between time, we still fight against spiritual forces and enemy ploys. Although sin and death have been defeated, in our flesh we still do battle. Jesus' Kingdom initiative has been inaugurated, but is not fully realized. And in this in-between time, one of the main ploys the Enemy uses against citizens in the West is to subtly encourage them to give in to the silent killers of apathy and fear.

Apathy continually tells us that we are OK... that we have done enough. We have done what we needed to do by initially trusting in Jesus, and now we can't really be bothered. Too many of us acknowledge Jesus on an intellectual level, but then it really just stops there. We think we have heaven in the bag, so what does it matter how we live our life or spend our time? We have bought into the culture and now just consume nicer or more wholesome things than we once did. Apathy allows us to try a few times to live this Kingdom life, but when results are not seen or frustration sets in, it tells us that it's not that big a deal and really isn't worth it. When people don't respond to our efforts or treat us poorly because of them, apathy lies us down and tells us it is no use. Our churches are filled with apathetic, tired, part-time citizens who are comfortable giving a little, but not sure about giving it all.

Fear tells us that we should be afraid of what we do not know or understand. We fear what we have not experienced or what we assume may happen to us if we continue on a certain path. Fear controls and manipulates. We are afraid of what may happen if we give up control. We fear not calling the shots in our own lives. We fear what could happen to our loved ones. We even fear change. In fact, fear can put a stranglehold on a person, a family, a group, or a church. It can get passed on like a virus and overwhelm a group till it paralyzes them. Once fear makes its home in an individual or a group, it is hard to shake it off.

I believe that both apathy and fear are enemies of the gospel. They are the spiritual vices of the comfortable churchgoer. They rob us of joy and trust in Jesus, and consequently disqualify us from living as ambassadors. They tell us to disengage with the world around us; to circle the wagons around our holy huddle of friends who look and act just like us, and not to venture out, because we don't know what might happen: "Stay in close where it is safe and known; plus, it's warm and comfortable in here." They harden our hearts, and then justify back to us that it is normal and OK. They do allow us to learn a lot about God, but are hell bent on not allowing what we learn to move into our hearts or actions. If you spend enough time under the lies of apathy and fear, you will soon be spiritually comatose.

Both apathy and fear are defeated foes.

You do not have to live under their bondage.

Reject the chains they bring and claim King Jesus' victory over them. You, citizen, do not have to be controlled by a spirit of fear or apathy. The King died so that you wouldn't have to deal with this any longer. They no longer claim mastery over you. Trust outshines fear, and intentionality outshines apathy – and the gospel freely offers us both.

So, where do we go from here? How do we live as citizens of the Kingdom within the constraints of our earthly responsibilities? What are the small changes that we can begin to make now so that we may grab hold of this life Jesus is calling us to?

As I hope has been made clear, it first of all requires a change in how you see yourself. You are an adopted son or daughter of the King. You are a citizen. You are a royal. You are chosen and loved immeasurably more than you can comprehend. You live for something eternal, something greater than this world can offer. The old you died, and now you are truly alive. You no longer have to live in bondage. You have a new and ultimate allegiance. You have GOD inside of you. You have been brought into a greater story, and been given a new role. You are no longer living as the main actor in your own drama. You have been forgiven and changed forever. The King has opened your heart. You have been supernaturally gifted. You have been transformed in order to transform. And now you are being sent out by the King as His ambassador and an initiator of His Kingdom.

This new way of seeing also allows you to view the world through the Kingdom lens. Choosing to leave the empires of the world behind and step into the alternative Kingdom is about seeing first and then doing. The colony is your lifeline. They are the alternative Kingdom people among whom you can know and be known, and through whom God will reveal more of Himself to you. You have the same identity and mission. Stay close to them.

Regarding your relationships, jobs, and responsibilities, ask yourself, "What does it look like for me to be a Kingdom bringer in this situation?" "In what small intentional ways can I live out my citizenship here?" "What is wrong here, and how can I be part of restoring *shalom*?" "What is not currently happening in my community that will be happening in the new heaven and new earth?" These are all areas in which there is an opportunity to go about working to restore *shalom*. Ask the Holy Spirit, "Please will You gently reveal to me what I am looking at in my world through the lens of the culture and not that of Your Kingdom? Will You give me the grace to make the necessary changes to put this right?"

Starting small and making decisive intentional steps toward this Kingdom way of life will bring honor to God and, in turn, bring joy to you and those you serve. You operate as an ambassador when your heart compels you and you willfully decide to engage with the lonely, live with an attitude of forgiveness, pursue reconciliation, and provide help for the physically afflicted; when you work at your job with diligence, when you show mercy and work for justice, as you proclaim the excellence of Christ, as you disadvantage yourself for others, as you speak with the stranger, as you parent faithfully, when you interact with others from a position of humility and not pride, and when you seek to make things right.

When the King finally returns and pours out absolute and never-ending *shalom* on all of creation, our mission as ambassadors will end. Satan will be defeated once and for all, and we citizens will enter the new Jerusalem. Everything will be made right. We will inherit the eternal Kingdom, and this glory that has been the deepest longing of our heart on this earth will now be ours.

John the apostle told us:

> And I saw the holy city – the new Jerusalem –
> descending out of heaven from God, made ready
> like a bride adorned for her husband. And I heard
> a loud voice from the throne saying: "Look! The
> residence of God is among human beings. He
> will live among them, and they will be his people,
> and God himself will be with them. He will wipe
> away every tear from their eyes, and death will
> not exist any more – or mourning, or crying, or
> pain, for the former things have ceased to exist."
> And the one seated on the throne said:
> "Look! I am making all things new!" Then he
> said to me, "Write it down, because these words
> are reliable and true." He also said to me, "It
> is done! I am the Alpha and the Omega, the

beginning and the end. To the one who is thirsty
I will give water free of charge from the spring
of the water of life. The one who conquers will
inherit these things, and I will be his God and he
will be my son."[144]

There will be no Temple because the Lord is the Temple
of the new city. There will be no sun or moon because the
glory of God will light everything in brilliance. The nations
will worship and God's light will shine on them, as He reigns
forever and ever.[145] It all started in a garden in Eden, and will
end in a glorious eternal city.

The King is inviting us into the greatest story imaginable.
This story is not yet complete, and you have been given
an invitation to join in and play a role as He unveils His
Kingdom. Jesus is enthroned in your life, and He is sending
you out to show the world what that looks like.

144 Revelation 21:2–7 (NET Bible™).
145 Revelation 22.

Benediction

A Sending Prayer

Father, have mercy on us.
Will You open our eyes to the beauty of You,
And in Your beauty may we find our joy.
Will You wake us from our slumber.
May You lift our heads until we see You clearly.
In Your gentleness, remind us of what You want
    from us,
Teach us what You require.
May You live deep within our hearts,
And give wisdom and discernment as to how we
    should live.
May we glorify You as citizens of Your Kingdom,
and represent You well on this earth.
You, O God, reign forever.
Bring Your reign and rule to our hearts and our
    hands.
May Your majesty and power propel us out
To live and love on earth as in heaven.

Amen.